SOCCER FITNESS

**More than 100 Drills
for Speed, Agility,
and Quickness**

ALAN PEARSON

Contemporary Books

Chicago New York San Francisco Lisbon London Madrid Mexico City
Milan New Delhi San Juan Seoul Singapore Sydney Toronto

Note: While every effort has been made to ensure that the content of this book is as technically accurate and as sound as possible, neither the author nor the publishers can accept responsibility for any injury or loss sustained as a result of the use of this material.

Metric to Imperial Conversions
1 centimeter (1 cm) = 0.394 inches
1 meter (m) = 1.094 yards
1 kilometer (km) = 1093.6 yards
1 kilogram (kg) = 2.205 pounds

This book was originally published by A&C Black Publishers Ltd., 37 Soho Square, London, W1D 3QZ.

Please see page 148 for trademark information.

3 4 5 6 7 8 9 0 FGR/FGR 2 1 0 9 8 7 6 5 4

ISBN 0-07-140690-5

Interior photographs courtesy of Pam Marshall.
Diagrams on pages 121–23 by Dave Saunders; all others courtesy of Angus Nicol and Carol Moore.

McGraw-Hill books are available at special quantity discounts to use as premiums and sales promotions, or for use in corporate training programs. For more information, please write to the Director of Special Sales, Professional Publishing, McGraw-Hill, Two Penn Plaza, New York, NY 10121-2298. Or contact your local bookstore.

This book is printed on acid-free paper.

Contents

Acknowledgments

A very special thank you to Pam Marshall, Peter Friar and the Leicester City F.C. Youth Academy. To Angus, Sarah, David and the rest of Team SAQ INTERNATIONAL, thank you for all your hard work.

A big thank you to Jonny and Nike U.K. for your support. Warm thanks to Steve Palmer, Graham Taylor and Craig Brown for your advice and support. Finally, my love and deepest thanks to my wife Silvana.

Alan Pearson
August 2001

Forewords

SAQ Training develops qualities that all soccer players should possess. In this well presented and easy to understand book, Alan Pearson links SAQ Training with soccer related exercises. None of the exercises are too complicated, thereby giving an excellent base for all coaches, trainers and players to work from.

Alan also demonstrates specific exercises for specific positions, enabling players to follow an individually designed SAQ Soccer Program if so desired.

Anyone who believes in helping players reach optimal fitness should have this book. I recommend it to all levels of the soccer world.

Graham Taylor
Football Manager
Lincoln City (1972–1977)
Watford (1977–1987)
Aston Villa (1987–1990)
England (1990–1993)
Wolverhampton Wanderers (1994–1995)
Watford (1996–2001)
Aston Villa (2002–   )

Having seen Alan Pearson at work, and having had the good fortune to listen to his invariably lucid and perceptive information on mobility, fitness and conditioning, I am pleased to note that he has, now, committed his thoughts to print.

Soccer Fitness will be a most useful resource for technicians in the game and will, I feel sure, have an undoubted impact on the overall fitness of players – from top international professionals to those indulging in the great game of soccer as a recreational activity.

Alan Pearson's well tried and carefully thought-out theories are to be commended.

Craig Brown
National Coach and Technical Director
Scottish Football Association

In the modern game of soccer, explosive pace and the ability to change direction quickly and accelerate instantly are of increasing importance. I believe that the practices of SAQ Training implemented within a soccer program over a period of time have a major impact on these areas.

The ideas and functional exercises and drills developed within the SAQ Program contribute to gaining the edge in a game where feet and inches can make all the difference between winning and losing.

Steve Palmer
Watford FC

Introduction

There is nothing more exhilarating than a player who explodes through a defensive gap, checks, turns and side-steps to avoid desperate, defensive lunges, and fires the ball home. Or when a center-half defies gravity by jumping into the air, hanging there long enough to intercept a crossed ball with his head before redirecting it to a supporting midfielder's feet for a swift, decisive counter-attack. Soccer is the greatest game in the world.

These wonderful acts of speed, agility and quickness are what make the difference between winning and losing. Often thought to be "God given" gifts, and therefore neglected on the training field, they are admired and believed to be essential for success within the game by players, managers, coaches and trainers.

The SAQ Program for soccer is the first ever soccer-specific program designed to develop these key skills. The program also has other significant benefits such as improving eye, hand and foot co-ordination, strength and explosive power, as well as being full of variety and great fun. The secret lies in the SAQ Continuum and the use of progressive, sequential learning techniques, breaking down complex sports science and making it easy to understand and practical to use. The end result is the development of multi-directional, explosive speed specifically for soccer. The program can be adapted to meet the needs of both squad training and of individual players within a squad who require position-specific development. It also provides an ideal opportunity for children as young as six, up to and including the most senior of professional players, to learn and improve.

The program has evolved from a foundation of years of practical experience out on the training fields of world soccer, talking to World Cup coaches, Premiership managers, élite and amateur players through to the little league players and school kids. This is what makes it so unique and in demand throughout the world. Many of Europe's top clubs now include SAQ Training as part of their everyday session, because it adds a new dimension to their preparation and also produces demonstrable results on the playing field.

This book allows coaches, trainers, managers and players to understand how and why SAQ Programs work. It provides clear, precise examples of how to put the theory into practice on the training ground. Its progressive structure even covers advanced, position-specific soccer drills that will allow you to integrate SAQ Training into all of your soccer training sessions.

What Is SAQ Training?

Speed has long been considered as just one single entity: how fast an object goes from point A to point B. Only recently has speed been studied and broken down into stages such as acceleration, the "plaining out" phase, deceleration, etc. Much of this research has been carried out by sports coaches involved in straight line running, so that the jumping, turning and zig-zagging speed necessary in soccer has been somewhat neglected.

Those involved with the development of SAQ Programs have sought to fill this void so as to develop all types of speed, particularly for team sports such as soccer. SAQ Programs break speed down into three main areas of skill: speed, agility and quickness. Although these may appear to be quite similar, they are in fact very different in terms of how they are trained, developed and integrated into a player's performance. When these skills are successfully combined and specialist SAQ Equipment is utilized, they provide the coach with the tools to make a good player into an outstanding one. It is remarkable what players can achieve with an SAQ Program.

Speed

A crucial part of any player's game is the ability to cover the ground efficiently and economically over the first few yards, and then to open up stride length and increase stride frequency when working over 40–50 yards. Speed means the maximum velocity a player can achieve and maintain; it can also be measured by the amount of time it takes a player to cover a particular distance. Most humans can only maintain maximum velocity for a short period of time or over a limited distance.

Training to improve maximum speed requires a great deal of focus on correct running mechanics, stride length and frequency, the leg cycle and hip-height/position. Drills such as the dead leg run and stride frequency drills that are used to help develop an economical running technique can all be easily integrated in a training session.

The best sprinters spend very little time in contact with the ground, and what contact they do make is extremely efficient and powerful. Focusing on the mechanics of running helps to control this power and use it efficiently and sparingly. Training when fresh is also crucial for an athlete/player to attain their maximum speed. Many athletes can only reproduce top speeds for a few weeks of the year, but the inclusion and practice of correct running mechanics on the training field will greatly benefit players in the game situation. How often have you seen a soccer player run as if they were playing a kettledrum – that is, with poor arm mechanics? Running like this will have a detrimental effect on the overall technique and, most importantly, the speed at which the player travels.

Agility

Agility is the ability to change direction without the loss of balance, strength, speed or body control. There is a direct link between improved agility and the development of an individual's timing, rhythm and movement.

Agility should not be taken for granted and can actually be taught to individual players. Training ensures that a player develops the best offensive and defensive skills possible with the greatest quickness, speed and control and the least amount of wasted energy and movement. Agility also has many other benefits for the individual, helping to prevent niggling injuries and teaching the muscles how to fire or activate properly and to control minute shifts in ankle, knee, hip, back, shoulder and neck joints for optimum body alignment.

Another very important benefit of agility training is that it is long-lasting. Unlike speed, stamina and weight training, it does not have to be maintained to retain the benefits. Consider the elderly person who can still ride a bicycle 40 years after having last ridden one. Agility training acts like an indelible mark, programming the body's memory of muscular movement patterns.

THE ELEMENTS OF AGILITY

There are four elements to agility:

- balance
- co-ordination
- programmed agility
- random agility

Within each of these there is also speed, strength, timing and rhythm.

Balance is a foundation of athleticism. Here the ability to stand, stop and walk is developed by focusing on the center of gravity, and it can be taught and retained relatively quickly. Examples include: standing on one leg, walking and standing on a balance beam, standing on an agility disc, walking backwards with your eyes closed, and jumping on a mini trampoline and then freezing. It does not take too long to train balance; it only requires a couple of minutes, two or three times a week, with the emphasis placed early in the morning and early in a training session when the players are fresh and alert. This is when the nervous system and muscles are more receptive to patterns of movement used in balance.

Co-ordination is the goal of mastering simple skills under more difficult stresses. Co-ordination work is often slow and methodical with an emphasis on correct biomechanics during athletically demanding movements. Training can be done by breaking a skill down into its component parts then gradually bringing them together. Co-ordination activities include footwork drills, tumbling, rolling and jumping. More difficult examples are walking on a balance beam while playing catch; running along a line while a partner lightly pulls and pushes in an attempt to move the player off the line; and jumping on and off an agility disc while holding a Jelly Ball.

The third element of agility training is called **"programmed" agility**. This is when a player has already experienced the skill or stress that is to be placed on them and is aware of the pattern and sequence of demands of that experience. In short, the player has already been programmed. Programmed agility drills can be conducted at high speeds but must be learnt at low, controlled speeds. Examples are zig-zag cone drills, shuttle runs and "T" cone drills, all of which involve change of direction along a known standardized pattern.

There is no spontaneity. Once these types of drills are learnt and performed on a regular basis, times and performances will improve and advances in strength, explosion, flexibility and body control will be experienced. This is true of players of any ability.

The final element – and the most difficult to master, prepare for and perform – is **random agility**. Here the player performs tasks with unknown patterns and unknown demands. The coach can incorporate visual and audible reactive skills so that the player has to make split-second decisions with movements based upon the various stimuli. The skill level is now becoming much closer to actual, game-like situations. Random agility can be trained by games like tag, read and react (tennis ball drops and dodge), dodge ball and more specific training such as jumping and landing followed by an immediate unknown movement demand from the coach.

Agility training is challenging, fun and exciting. There is the opportunity for tremendous variety, and training should not become boring or laborious. Agility is not just for those with elite sporting abilities – try navigating through a busy shopping mall!

Quickness

When a player accelerates, a great deal of force has to be generated and transferred through the foot to the ground. This action is similar to that when you roll a towel up (the "leg"), hold one end in your hand and flick it out to achieve a "cracking" noise from the other end (the "foot"). The act of acceleration occurs in a fraction of a second and takes the body from a static position to motion. Muscles actually lengthen and then shorten instantaneously – that is, an "eccentric" followed by a "concentric" contraction. This process is known as the stretch shortening cycle (SCC) action. SAQ Training concentrates on improving the neuro-muscular system that impacts on this process, so that this initial movement – whether lateral (to the side), linear (in a straight line) or vertical (upwards) – is automatic, explosive and precise. The reaction time is the time it takes for the brain to receive and respond to a stimulus by sending a message to the muscle, causing it to contract. This is what helps a soccer player to cut right – left – right again and then burn down the sideline, or a goalkeeper to make a split-second reaction save. With ongoing SAQ Training, the neuro-muscular system is reprogrammed and restrictive mental blocks and thresholds such as slow, unco-ordinated initial acceleration and limited range of movement are removed or improved. Consequently, messages from the brain have a clear path to the muscles so that the result is an instinctively quicker player.

Quickness training begins with "innervation" (isolated fast contractions of an individual joint): for example, repeating the same explosive movement over a short period of time, such as fast feet and line drills. These quick, repetitive motions take the body through the gears, moving it in a co-ordinated manner to develop speed. Integrating quickness training throughout the year by using fast feet and reaction-type drills will result in the muscles having increased firing rates. This means that players are capable of faster, more controlled acceleration. The goal is to ensure that players "explode" over the first 3–5 yards. Imagine that the firing between the nervous system and the muscles are the gears in a car; the timing, speed and smoothness of the gear-change dictates whether or not the wheels, and thus the car, accelerate away efficiently – with balance and co-ordination, so that the wheels do not spin and the car does not lose control.

Movement Skills

Many elements of balance and co-ordination involve the processing of sensory information from within the body. Proprioceptors are sensors that detect muscular tension, tension in tendons, relative body positions and pressure in the skin. In addition, the body has a range of other sensors that detect balance. The ability to achieve balance and co-ordination is highly dependent on the effectiveness of the body's internal sensors and proprioceptors, just like the suspension on a car. Through training, these sensors, and the neural communication system within the body, become more effective. In addition, the brain becomes more able to interpret these messages and formulate the appropriate movement response. This physiological development underpins effective movement and future movement skill development.

SAQ Equipment

SAQ Equipment adds variety and stimuli to your training session. Drill variations are almost endless and once mastered, the results achieved can be quite astonishing. Players of all ages and abilities enjoy the challenges presented to them when training with SAQ Equipment, particularly when introduced in a soccer-specific manner.

When using SAQ Equipment, coaches, trainers and players must be aware of the safety issues involved – and of the reduced effectiveness and potentially dangerous consequence of using inappropriate or inferior equipment. Having said this, many of the drills can be performed using equipment that is readily available to most coaches – such as cones, garden canes and so on – always provided that safety and correct technique remain priorities. The following pages introduce a variety of SAQ Equipment recommended for use in many of the drills detailed later in this book.

FAST FOOT LADDERS

These are made of webbing with round, hard plastic rungs spaced approximately 18 inches apart. They come in sets of two pieces, each measuring 15 feet. The pieces can be joined together or used as two separate ladders; they can also be folded over to create different angles for players to perform drills on. Fast Foot Ladders are great for improving agility and for the development of explosive fast feet.

MICRO AND MACRO HURDLES

These come in two sizes; micro hurdles measuring 7 inches and macro hurdles measuring 12 inches in height. They are constructed of a hard plastic and have been specifically designed as a safe, free-standing piece of equipment. It is recommended that the hurdles be used in sets of 6–8 to perform the mechanics drills detailed later. They are ideal for practicing running mechanics and low-impact plyometrics. The Micro Hurdles are also great for lateral work.

SONIC CHUTES

These are constructed from webbing (the belt), nylon cord and a lightweight cloth "chute," the size of which may vary from 5–6 feet. The belts have a release mechanism that when pulled, drops the chute so that the player can explode forwards. These are great for developing sprint endurance.

VIPER BELT

This is a resistance belt specially made for high-intensity training. It has three stainless steel anchor points where a flexi-cord can be attached. The flexi-cord is made from surgical tubing with a specific elongation. The Viper Belt has a safety belt and safety fasteners; it is double-stitched and provides a good level of resistance. This piece of equipment is useful for developing explosive speed in all directions.

SIDE-STEPPERS

These are padded ankle straps that are connected together by an adjustable flexi cord. They are useful for the development of lateral movements.

REACTION BALL

A rubber ball specifically shaped so that it bounces in unpredictable directions.

OVERSPEED TOW ROPE

This is made up of two belts and a 50-yard nylon cord pulley system. It can be used to provide resistance and is specifically designed for the development of express overspeed and swerve running.

BREAK-AWAY BELT

This is a webbing belt that is connected by Velcro-covered connecting strips. It is great for mirror drills and position-specific marking drills, breaking apart when one player gets away from the other.

STRIDE FREQUENCY CANES

Plastic, 4-foot canes of different colors that are used to mark out stride patterns.

SPRINT SLED

A metal Sled with a center area to accommodate different weights and a running harness that is attached by webbing straps of 8–10 yards in length.

JELLY BALLS

Round, soft rubber balls filled with a water-based "jelly like" substance. They come in different weights from 4–18 lb. They differ from the old-fashioned medicine balls because they can be bounced with great force on to hard surfaces.

HAND WEIGHTS

Foam-covered weights, each weighing 1.5–2.5 lb. They are safe and easy to use both indoors and outdoors.

VISUAL ACUITY RING

A hard plastic ring of approx. 30 inches in diameter with four different colored balls attached to it, all equally distributed around the ring. The ring helps to develop visual acuity and tracking skills when thrown and caught between the players. This piece of equipment is particularly good for goalkeepers.

PERIPHERAL VISION STICK

The stick is simple but very effective for the training of peripheral vision. It is approximately 4 feet long with a brightly colored ball at one end. Once again, this is effective for all players and particularly good for goalkeepers.

BUNT BAT

A 4-foot stick with three colored balls – one at each end and one in the middle. Working in pairs player 1 holds the bat with two hands while player 2 throws a small ball or bean bag for player 1 to "bunt" or fend off. Useful for all players, but particularly useful in developing goalkeepers' hand–eye co-ordination.

AGILITY DISC

An inflatable rubber disc 18 inches across. The discs are multi-purpose but particularly good for proprio-receptive and core development work (to strengthen the deep muscles of the trunk). They can be stood on, kneeled on, sat on and laid on for the performance of all types of exercises.

The SAQ Continuum

Many games activities are characterized by explosive movements, acceleration and deceleration, agility,

turning ability and speed of responses (Smythe 2000). The SAQ Continuum is the sequence and progression of components that make up a SAQ Training Session. The progressive elements include soccer-specific patterns of running and drills including ball work. The continuum is also flexible, and once the pre-season foundation work has been completed, during the season – when time and recovery are of the essence – short-combination SAQ Training Sessions provide a constant top-up to the skills that have already been learned.

SAQ Training is like any other fitness training – if neglected, then players' explosive, multi-directional power will diminish. The component parts of the SAQ Continuum and how they relate to soccer are as follows:

- **Dynamic Flex** – warm-up on the move
- **mechanics of movement** – the development of running form for soccer
- **innervation** – fast feet, agility and control for soccer
- **accumulation of potential** – the bringing together of the previous components in a SAQ Training Soccer Circuit
- **explosion** – the development of explosive, three-step multi-directional acceleration for soccer
- **expression of potential** – short, competitive team games that prepare the players for the next level of training
- **warm-down**

Throughout the continuum, position-specific drills and skills can be implemented.

CHAPTER 1 DYNAMIC FLEX

WARM-UP ON THE MOVE

It is common knowledge that, before engaging in intense or strenuous exercise, the body should be prepared. The warm-up should achieve a change in a number of physiological responses, in order that the body can work safely and effectively:

- increase the body temperature, specifically core (deep) muscle temperature
- increase the heart rate and blood flow
- increase the breathing rate
- increase the elasticity of muscular tissues
- activate the neuro-muscular system
- increase mental alertness

The warm-up should take a performer from a rested state to the physiological state required for participation in the session that is to follow. It should gradually increase in intensity as the session goes on. In addition, the warm-up should be fun and stimulating for the players, "switching them on" mentally.

What Is Dynamic Flex?

The standard training session for soccer begins by warming the players up before taking them through a series of stretches that focus on the main muscle groups in the body. However, "static" stretches like this are not really relevant within a game of soccer. Players do not need to be able to do the splits like gymnasts and dancers, but they do need to be able to perform an overhead kick or a side-on volley. Dynamic Flex is what allows a soccer player to do this: flexibility in action, if you like, combined with power and strength.

Indeed, the most recent research has shown that static stretching before training or competition can actually be detrimental to performance. One study found that the eccentric strength of the muscle – its strength when lengthening, for instance when a player brakes or lands from a jump – was reduced by 7–9% for up to an hour after static stretching. Similarly, it was discovered that there was a clear decrease in the peak power output of the muscle after stretching.

Dynamic stretching, on the other hand, has been shown to increase muscle warmth, and therefore its elasticity. This is vital for performance and muscle safety. Indeed, one of the main arguments in favor of static stretching – that it helps to prevent injury – has also now been called into question. Recent research suggests that static stretching has almost no effect on this (Gleim & McHugh 1997). Similarly, an Australian army physiotherapist (Pope, 1999) studied army recruits over the course of a year. He instructed half to warm up with static stretching and half to warm up without any stretching at all. He found no differences in the incidence of injury between the two groups, suggesting that static stretching is of little benefit in the pre-exercise warm-up.

The Warm–Up

This uses a standard grid of 20×20 yard (*see* fig. 1.1 overleaf). The following exercises represent a foundation set of Dynamic Flex warm-up drills. Also included in this chapter are variations and the introduction of the ball.

It is important to remember that soccer players not only enjoy variety but also respond proactively on the field to variations in training. Once they have mastered the standard set, the introduction of new grids (*see* figs 1.2–1.6) and combination work including the ball will ensure maximum participation.

In a warm-up drill, start slow, rehearse the
movements then increase the intensity.

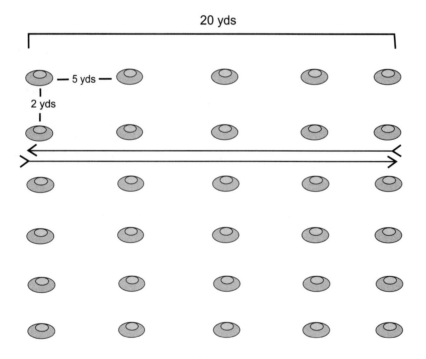

Figure 1.1 Standard grid

Key

Direction of running

DRILL — WALKING ON THE BALLS OF THE FEET

Aim
To stretch shins and improve ankle mobility. To improve balance and co-ordination. To increase body temperature.

Area/equipment
An indoor or outdoor grid 20 yards in length. The width of the grid is variable depending on the size of the squad (*see* fig. 1.1).

Description
Player to cover the length of the grid by walking on the balls of the feet. Return to the start by repeating the drill in a backward motion.

Key teaching points
- Do not walk on the ends of the toes
- Keep off the heels
- Maintain correct arm mechanics (*see* page 30)
- Maintain an upright posture

Sets and reps
2 × 20 yards, 1 forwards and 1 backwards.

Variations/progressions
Perform the drill laterally (in a sideways motion) but do not allow the feet to come together completely. Push off with the back foot, do not pull with the lead foot.

DRILL ANKLE FLICKS

Aim

To stretch calves and improve ankle mobility. To improve balance, co-ordination and rhythm of movement. To prepare for good foot-to-floor contact. To increase body temperature.

Area/equipment

An indoor or outdoor grid 20 yards in length. The width of the grid is variable depending on the size of the squad (*see* fig. 1.1).

Description

Player to cover the length of the grid in a "skipping"-type motion, in which the balls of the feet plant then flick up towards the shins. The player should be seen to move in a bouncing manner. Return to the start by repeating the drill in a backward motion.

Key teaching points

- Work off the ball of the foot – not the toes
- Practice the first few steps on the spot before moving off
- Maintain correct arm mechanics (*see* page 30)
- Maintain an upright posture

Sets and reps

2 × 20 yards, 1 forwards and 1 backwards.

Variations/progressions

Perform the drill laterally.

DRILL   *SMALL SKIPS*

Aim
To improve lower leg flexibility and ankle mobility. To improve balance, co-ordination and rhythm, and develop positive foot-to-ground contact. To increase body temperature.

Area/equipment
An indoor or outdoor grid 20 yards in length. The width of the grid is variable depending on the size of the squad (*see* fig. 1.1).

Description
Player to cover the length of the grid in a low skipping motion. Return to the start by repeating the drill in a backward motion.

Key teaching points
- Knee to be raised to an angle of approximately 45–55°
- Work off the ball of the foot
- Maintain correct arm mechanics (*see* page 30)
- Maintain an upright posture
- Maintain a good rhythm

Sets and reps
2 × 20 yards, 1 forwards and 1 backwards.

Variations/progressions
Perform the drill laterally.

DRILL WIDE SKIP

Aim
To increase hip and ankle mobility. To improve balance, co-ordination and rhythm. To increase body temperature.

Area/equipment
An indoor or outdoor grid 20 yards in length. The width of the grid is variable depending on the size of the squad (*see* fig. 1.1).

Description
Player to cover the length of the grid by skipping. The feet should remain shoulder-width apart and the knees face outwards at all times. Return to the start by repeating the drill in a backward motion.

Key teaching points
- Keep off the heels
- Maintain correct arm mechanics (*see* page 30)
- Maintain an upright posture
- Do not take the thigh above a 90° angle

Sets and reps
2 × 20 yards, 1 forwards and 1 backwards.

Variations/progressions
Perform the drill laterally.

DRILL   SINGLE-KNEE DEAD-LEG LIFT

Aim
To improve buttock flexibility and hip mobility. To isolate the correct "running cycle" motion for each leg.

Area/equipment
An indoor or outdoor grid 20 yards in length. The width of the grid is variable depending on the size of the squad (*see* fig. 1.1).

Description
Player to cover the length of the grid by bringing the knee of one leg quickly up to a 90° position. The other leg should remain as straight as possible with a very short lift away from the ground throughout the movement. The ratio should be 1:4 – i.e. 1 lift to every 4 steps, working one leg on the way down the grid and the other on the return.

Key teaching points
■ Do not take the knee above a 90° angle
■ Strike the floor with the ball of the foot
■ Keep the foot facing forwards
■ Maintain correct running mechanics (*see* pages 29–31)

Sets and reps
2 × 20 yards, 1 forwards and 1 backwards.

Variations/progressions
Vary the lift ratio, e.g 1:2.

DRILL HIGH KNEE-LIFT SKIP

Aim
To improve buttock flexibility and hip mobility. To increase the Range of Motion (ROM) over a period of time. To develop rhythm. To increase body temperature.

Area/equipment
An indoor or outdoor grid 20 yards in length. The width of the grid is variable depending on the size of the squad (*see* fig. 1.1).

Description
Player to cover the length of the grid in a high skipping motion. Return to the start by repeating the drill in a backward motion.

Key teaching points
- Thigh to be taken past 90°
- Work off the balls of the feet
- Maintain a strong core
- Maintain an upright posture
- Control the head by looking forwards at all times
- Maintain correct arm mechanics (*see* page 30)

Sets and reps
2 × 20 yards, 1 forwards and 1 backwards.

Variations/progressions
Perform the drill laterally.

DRILL KNEE-ACROSS SKIP

Aim
To improve outer hip flexibility and hip mobility over a period of time. To develop balance and co-ordination. To increase body temperature.

Area/equipment
An indoor or outdoor grid 20 yards in length. The width of the grid is variable depending on the size of the squad (*see* fig. 1.1).

Description
Player to cover the length of the grid in a skipping motion, bringing the knee across the body. Return to the start by repeating the drill in a backward motion.

Key teaching points
- Do not force an increased ROM
- Work off the balls of the feet
- Maintain a strong core
- Maintain an upright posture
- Control the head by looking forwards at all times
- Use the arms primarily for balance

Sets and reps
2 × 20 yards, 1 forwards and 1 backwards.

Variations/progressions
Perform the drill laterally.

DRILL *LATERAL RUNNING*

Aim
To develop an economical knee drive. To stretch the quadriceps and prepare for an efficient lateral running technique. To increase body temperature.

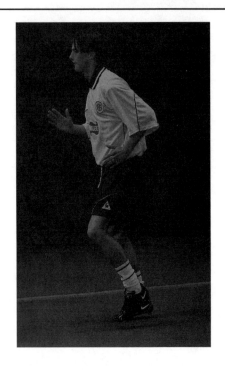

Area/equipment
An indoor or outdoor grid 20 yards in length. The width of the grid is variable depending on the size of the squad (*see* fig. 1.1).

Description
Player to cover the length of the grid with the left or right shoulder leading, taking short lateral steps. Return with the opposite shoulder leading.

Key teaching points
- Keep the hips square
- Work off the balls of the feet
- Do not skip
- Do not let the feet cross over
- Maintain an upright posture
- Do not sink into the hips (*see* page 30) or bend over at the waist
- Do not overstride – use short sharp steps
- Maintain correct arm mechanics (*see* page 30)

Sets and reps
2 × 20 yards, 1 left shoulder lead and 1 right shoulder lead.

Variations/progressions
Practice lateral-angled zig-zag runs.

DRILL   *KNEE-OUT SKIP*

Aim
To stretch the inner thigh and improve hip mobility. To develop an angled knee drive, balance, co-ordination and rhythm. To increase body temperature.

Area/equipment
An indoor or outdoor grid 20 yards in length. The width of the grid is variable depending on the size of the squad (*see* fig. 1.1).

Description
Player to cover the length of the grid in a skipping motion. The knees move from the center of the body to a lateral position, "outside" the body, before returning to the central position. Return to the start by repeating the drill in a backward motion.

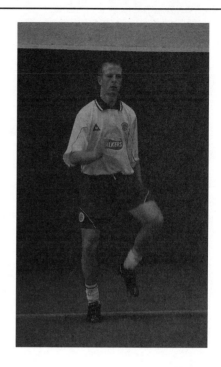

Key teaching points
■ Feet start facing forwards and move outwards as the knees are raised
■ Work off the balls of the feet
■ The knee is to be pushed out and back, not rolled out
■ Maintain correct arm mechanics (*see* page 30)
■ The movement should be smooth and not jerky

Sets and reps
2 × 20 yards, 1 forwards and 1 backwards.

Variations/progressions
Perform the drill laterally.

DRILL   PRE-TURN

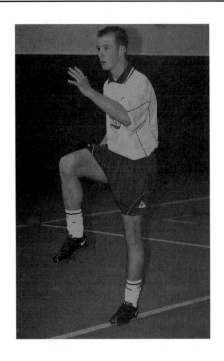

Aim
To prepare the hips for a turning action without committing the whole body. To increase body temperature. To improve body control.

Area/equipment
An indoor or outdoor grid 20 yards in length. The width of the grid is variable depending on the size of the squad (*see* fig. 1.1).

Description
Player to cover the length of the grid by performing a lateral movement. The heel of the back foot is moved to a position almost alongside the lead foot. Just before the feet come together, the lead foot is moved away sideways. Return to the start by repeating the drill but lead with the opposite shoulder.

Key teaching points
- The back foot must not cross the lead foot
- Work off the balls of the feet
- Maintain correct arm mechanics (*see* page 30)
- Maintain an upright posture
- Do not sink into the hips or fold at the waist (*see* page 30)
- Do not use a high knee lift; the angle should be below 90° and preferably no more than 45°

Sets and reps
2 × 20 yards, 1 left shoulder leading and 1 right shoulder leading.

DRILL   *RUSSIAN WALK*

Aim
To stretch the back of thighs. To improve hip mobility and ankle stabilization. To develop balance and co-ordination. To increase body temperature.

Area/equipment
An indoor or outdoor grid 20 yards in length. The width of the grid is variable depending on the size of the squad (*see* fig. 1.1).

Description
Player to cover the length of the grid by performing a walking march with a high extended step. Imagine that the aim is to scrape the sole of your shoe down the front of a door.

Key teaching points
- Lift the knee before extending the leg
- Work off the balls of the feet
- Try to keep off the heels, particularly on the back foot
- Keep the hips square

Sets and reps
2 × 20 yards, both forwards.

Variations/progressions
Perform the drill backwards.

DRILL *WALKING LUNGE*

Aim

To stretch the front of the hips and thighs. To develop balance and co-ordination. To increase body temperature.

Area/equipment

An indoor or outdoor grid 20 yards in length. The width of the grid is variable depending on the size of the squad (*see* fig. 1.1).

Description

Player to cover the length of the grid by performing a walking lunge. The front leg should be bent with a 90° angle at the knee and the thigh in a horizontal position. The back leg should also be at a 90° angle but with the knee touching the ground and the thigh in a vertical position. Return to the start by repeating the drill in a backward motion.

Key teaching points

- Try to keep the hips square
- Maintain a strong core and keep upright
- Maintain good control
- Persevere with backward lunges – these are difficult to master

Sets and reps

2 × 20 yards, 1 forwards and 1 backwards.

Variations/progressions

- Perform the drill with hand weights
- Perform the drill while catching and passing a ball in the lunge position

DRILL SIDE LUNGE

Aim
To stretch the inner thighs and gluteals (buttocks). To develop balance and co-ordination. To increase body temperature.

Area/equipment
An indoor or outdoor grid 20 yards in length. The width of the grid is variable depending on the size of the squad (*see* fig. 1.1).

Description
Player to cover the length of the grid by performing lateral lunges. Take a wide lateral step and simultaneously lower the gluteals towards the ground. Return to the start with the opposite shoulder leading.

Key teaching points
- Do not bend at the waist or lean forwards
- Try to keep off the heels
- Maintain a strong core
- Use the arms primarily for balance

Sets and reps
2 × 20 yards, 1 left shoulder leading and 1 right shoulder leading.

Variations/progressions
Work in pairs facing each other and chest-passing the ball.

DRILL   *HURDLE WALK*

Aim
To stretch the inner and outer thighs, and increase ROM. To develop balance and co-ordination. To increase body temperature.

Area/equipment
An indoor or outdoor grid 20 yards in length. The width of the grid is variable depending on the size of the squad (*see* fig. 1.1).

Description
Player to cover the length of the grid by walking in a straight line and alternating the lifting leg as if going over a high hurdle. Return to the start by repeating the drill in a backward motion.

Key teaching points
■ Try to keep the body square as the hips rotate
■ Work off the balls of the feet
■ Maintain an upright posture
■ Do not sink into the hips or bend over at the waist (*see* page 30)
■ Imagine that you are actually stepping over a barrier

Sets and reps
2 × 20 yards, 1 forwards and 1 backwards.

DRILL *WALKING HAMSTRING*

Aim
To stretch the backs of the thighs. To increase body temperature.

Area/equipment
An indoor or outdoor grid 20 yards in length. The width of the grid is variable depending on the size of the squad (*see* fig. 1.1).

Description
Player to cover the length of the grid by extending the lead leg heel first on to the ground and rolling on to the ball of the foot. Walk forwards and repeat on the opposite leg. Continue in this manner, alternating the lead leg.

Key teaching points
- Keep the spine in a straight line
- Do not arch the back but lean into the stretch from the hips (*see* photo)
- Control the head by looking forwards at all times
- Work at a steady pace, do not rush

Sets and reps
2 × 20 yards, 1 forwards and 1 backwards.

DRILL *HAMSTRING BUTTOCK FLICKS*

Aim
To stretch the front and back of the thighs. To improve hip mobility. To increase body temperature.

Area/equipment
An indoor or outdoor grid 20 yards in length. The width of the grid is variable depending on the size of the squad (*see* fig. 1.1).

Description
Player to cover the length of the grid by moving forwards, alternating leg flicks with the heel moving up towards the buttocks. Return to the start by repeating the drill in a backward motion.

Key teaching points
- Start slowly and build up the tempo
- Work off the balls of the feet
- Maintain an upright posture
- Do not sink into the hips
- Try to develop a rhythm

Sets and reps
2 × 20 yards, 1 forwards and 1 backwards.

Variations/progressions
- Perform the drill laterally
- Perform the drill as above but flick the heel to the outside of the buttocks

DRILL CARIOCA

Aim
To improve hip mobility and speed, which will increase the firing of nerve impulses over a period of time. To develop balance and co-ordination whilst moving and twisting. To increase body temperature.

Area/equipment
An indoor or outdoor grid 20 yards in length. The width of the grid is variable depending on the size of the squad (*see* fig. 1.1).

Description
Player to cover the length of the grid by moving laterally. The rear foot crosses in front of the body and then moves around to the back of the body. Simultaneously, the lead foot will do the opposite. The arms also move across the front and back of the body.

Key teaching points
- Start slowly and build up the tempo
- Work off the balls of the feet
- Keep the shoulders square
- Do not force the ROM
- Use the arms primarily for balance

Sets and reps
2 × 20 yards, 1 left leg leading and 1 right leg leading.

Variations/progressions
Perform the drill with a partner (mirror drills) – i.e. one initiates/leads the movement while the other attempts to follow.

DRILL   WALL DRILL – LEG ACROSS BODY

Aim
To increase the ROM in the hip region. To increase body temperature.

Area/equipment
A wall or fence to lean against.

Description
The player faces and leans against the wall or fence at an angle of approximately 20–30°. One leg is taken out to the side of the body and then swung across it. Repeat on the other leg.

Key teaching points
- Do not force an increased ROM
- Work off the balls of the feet
- Lean with both hands against the wall or fence
- Keep the hips square
- Do not look down
- Gradually increase the speed of the movement

Sets and reps
7–10 on each leg. Players to work one leg and then alternate.

Variations/progressions
Lean against a partner as shown – but being careful how the leg is swung!

DRILL   *WALL DRILL – FORWARD LEG SWING*

Aim
To increase the ROM in the hip region. To increase body temperature.

Area/equipment
A wall or fence to lean against.

Description
The player faces and leans against the wall or fence at an angle of approximately 20–30°. Take the leg back and swing it forwards in a linear motion along the same plane. Repeat on the other leg.

Key teaching points
- Do not force an increased ROM
- Work off the balls of the feet
- Lean with both hands against the wall or fence
- Do not look down
- Gradually increase the speed of the movement

Sets and reps
7–10 on each leg. Players to work one leg and then alternate.

Variations/progressions
Lean against a partner as shown – being careful how the leg is swung!

DRILL   WALL DRILL – KNEE ACROSS BODY

Aim
To increase the ROM in the hip region. To increase body temperature.

Area/equipment
A wall or fence to lean against.

Description
The player faces and leans against the wall or fence at an angle of approximately 20–30°. From a standing position, drive one knee upwards and across the body. Repeat on the other leg.

Key teaching points
- Do not force an increased ROM
- Work off the ball of the support foot
- Lean with both hands against the wall or fence
- Keep the hips square
- Do not look down
- Gradually increase the speed of the movement
- Imagine you are trying to get your knee up and across the body to the opposite hip region

Sets and reps
7–10 on each leg. Players to work one leg and then alternate.

Variations/progressions
Lean against a partner as shown – being careful how you raise your knee!

DRILL   *PAIR DRILL – LATERAL RUNS*

Aim
To develop running skills in a more game-specific situation. To stimulate balance, co-ordination. To practice the reassertion of the correct mechanics from an imbalanced position. To increase body temperature.

Area/equipment
An indoor or outdoor grid 20 yards in length. The width of the grid is variable depending on the size of the squad.

Description
The players face each other approximately 2–3 feet apart and cover the length of the grid sideways taking short lateral steps. Occasionally one can push the other.

Key teaching points
- *See* lateral running (page 10)
- When off balance or after being pushed, the focus should be on the reassertion of the correct arm and foot mechanics

Sets and reps
2 × 20 yards, 1 left leg leading and 1 right leg leading.

Variations/progressions
Introduce the ball and pass hand-to-hand and then hand-to-foot.

DRILL PAIR DRILL – JOCKEYING

Aim
To simulate defensive and attacking close-quarter movement patterns.
To increase body temperature.

Area/equipment
An indoor or outdoor grid 20 yards in length. The width of the grid is
variable depending on the size of the squad.

Description
Players stand facing each other and cover the grid working both
forwards and backwards. The player moving forwards (attacker)
shows his left shoulder and then his right shoulder alternately in a
rhythmic motion. The player moving backwards (defender) mirrors
the attacking player's movements.

Key teaching points
■ Take short steps
■ Do not cross the feet
■ Maintain a strong core and an upright posture
■ Do not sink into the hips (*see* page 30)
■ Keep your eyes on the opponent at all times

Sets and reps
2 × 20 yards, 1 left leg leading and 1 right leg leading.

Variations/progressions
Introduce the ball to the attacking player who presses with the ball at
their feet, transferring it from left to right to keep the defender on their
toes.

DRILL   *SPRINTS*

Aim
To increase the intensity of the warm-up and prepare players for maximum exertion. To speed up the firing rate of neuro-muscular messages. To increase body temperature.

Area/equipment
An indoor or outdoor grid 20 yards in length. The width of the grid is variable depending on the size of the squad. Sprint one way only; perform a jog-back recovery on the outside of the grid.

Description
Players to start from different angles – e.g. side-on, backwards, etc. – and to accelerate into a forward running motion down the grid.

Key teaching points
- Maintain good running mechanics (*see* pages 29–31)
- Ensure that players alternate the lead foot

Sets and reps
1 set of 5 sprints, varying the start position.

Variations/progressions
- Include swerving sprints
- Include turns in the sprints

GRID VARIATIONS

Grid variations can be used to challenge and stimulate the players with a variety of movement patterns. These variations help to prevent players from becoming over-familiar with drills, which often leads to complacency. The following grid variations are examples only – feel free to use your imagination and design your own.

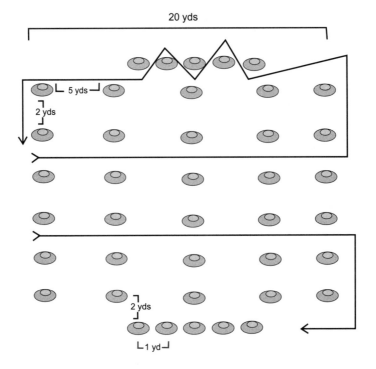

Figure 1.2 Grid variation

GRID VARIATIONS

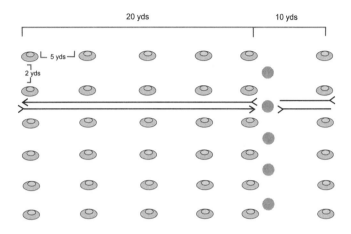

Figure 1.3 Split grid

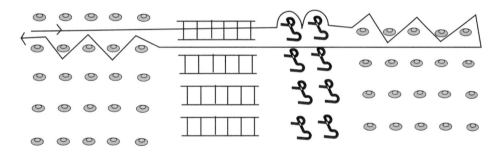

Figure 1.4 Combination warm-up grid 1

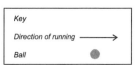

Key

Direction of running ⟶

Ball ●

GRID VARIATIONS

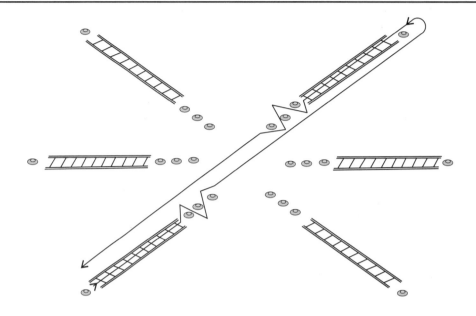

Figure 1.5 Combination warm-up grid 2 – multi-crossover

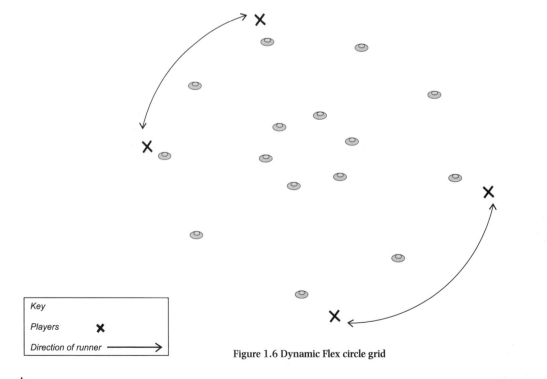

Key

Players   ✗

Direction of runner ⟶

Figure 1.6 Dynamic Flex circle grid

CHAPTER 2 SOCCER RUNNING FORM

THE MECHANICS OF MOVEMENT

Do not take it for granted that players have been taught how to run correctly, or that it is something which occurs naturally. You will always encounter natural, "genetically gifted" players who are explosive and who make running quickly look easy – although these are few and far between. To neglect running mechanics in your soccer training is to ignore the potential in many of your players. How often do you hear comments like "good player but slow," "falls back on his heels" or "not quick enough over the first few yards"? All players, whatever their age, can improve their speed and acceleration by using and practicing the correct running mechanics.

The best players and teams in the world are able to vary the pace of their play effectively. They inject explosive phases and controlled deceleration, allowing them to constantly vary the speed of the game to suit the situation. Indeed, the demands of the game are continually changing. Recent research provides the following statistics on time spent performing various movements in a game of soccer:

walking/standing	28%	(4 km/h)
jogging	26%	(8 km/h)
running – low speed	21%	(12 km/h)
running – moderate	14%	(16 km/h)
running – high	6%	(21 km/h)
running – sprint	3%	(30 km/h)
running – backwards	2%	

Soccer players do not run continuously at the same pace. In the course of a game, they perform more than 1000 changes in activity and use over 420 different patterns of movement. The ball is in play for less than 60 minutes out of the whole match, with average bursts of activity of 4–6 seconds over distances of 20–25 yards. On average a player will touch the ball for less than 2 minutes per game. A forward will sprint more than a midfielder, who will cover a greater distance (World Cup, personal communication 1998).

All these statistics highlight the importance of correct mechanics in running, which in turn impacts on an individual's economy of movement and effectiveness in covering the ground.

There is no need to focus on the techniques required for the 100 m sprint. Players very rarely have the space to plain out (maximum maintainable speed) after 30 m or relax and think about "jelly jaw" techniques! Instead, soccer requires a sound basic technique, together with the ability to change from correct running mechanics to holding off a player, using the arms for balance with the ball at the feet, and then reasserting good mechanics to re-accelerate.

The player who can explode over the first few yards will always be the one in front. I will never forget an interview with Mickey Quinn of Coventry City, who was famous for his large frame and ample stomach, yet who was top scorer in the Premiership. When asked how he did it, his reply was that he was the quickest over the first 5 yards.

The first 5 yards are crucial because this is when a great deal of energy, force and power are used to propel the body forwards. During this initial phase (the acceleration phase), emphasis should be placed on a short stride length and a high stride frequency. As the player accelerates stride length will increase and stride frequency will decrease resulting in the player covering a greater distance with each stride until they achieve maximum speed. Correct stride length and frequency are vital for effective and efficient running.

ARM MECHANICS

Good soccer running form is not all about leg work. Power and balance come from the upper body, so encourage the following techniques in your players.

- elbows should be held at 90°
- hands and shoulders should be relaxed
- the inside of the wrist should brush against your pockets
- the hands should move from the buttock cheeks to the chest or head.

Lift Mechanics

Soccer is a multi-sprint, stop-and-start sport, so the first phase of acceleration and re-acceleration is crucial. Coaching players to get their knees up high, particularly in the first few yards of the acceleration phase, only makes them slower. It has the negative effect of minimizing force development, so that insufficient power is produced to propel the body forwards in an explosive action.

During the first few yards of acceleration, short, sharp steps are actually required. These generate a high degree of force which takes the body from a stationary position into the first controlled explosive steps. Look and listen for the following in a player's initial acceleration strides:

- 45° knee-lift
- knees coming up in a vertical line
- front of the foot stays in a linear (forward-facing) position
- on the lift, the foot will transfer from pointing slightly down to pointing slightly up
- if the foot or the knee splays in or out, this means that power will not be transferred correctly

- foot-to-floor contact with the ball of the foot
- keep off the heels
- foot-to-floor contact makes a tapping noise, not a thud or a slap

Posture

Posture is also an important part of acceleration and sprinting. The spine should be kept as straight as possible at all times. This means that a player who has tackled, jockeyed or jumped for the ball and now needs to run into space, needs to transfer to the correct running form as quickly as possible. Running with a straight spine does not mean running bolt upright; you can keep your spine straight using a slight forward lean. What *is* to be avoided is players "sinking into their hips," which looks like running "folded up in the middle," because this prevents effective transfer of power.

Mechanics for Deceleration

The ability of a player to stop quickly, change direction and accelerate away from an opponent is a key area in building successful teams. You can practice this: do not leave it to chance; include it in your sessions.

- *Posture* – lean back. This alters the angle of the spine and hips which control foot placement. Foot contact with the ground will now transfer to the heel, which acts like a brake.
- *Fire the arms* – by firing the arms quickly, the energy produced will increase the frequency of heel contact to the ground. Think of it like pressing harder on the brakes in a car.

The running techniques described in this chapter cover basic mechanics for soccer-specific techniques, where running, pushing, jumping and turning are all important parts of the game. These are developed through the use of hurdles, stride frequency canes and running technique drills.

Mechanics for Jumping

As with running, arm drive is crucial for an efficient jumping technique. Both arms should move together through an arc from the hips to the ears in an explosive, upward, driving motion. This technique raises the body's center of gravity – transferring a downward force through the hips and legs into an upward force that enables maximal upward thrust. The art is to maintain an upright position, use only a slight bend at the knees and simultaneously power off the balls of the feet. It is important to remember not to sink too deep into the hips on landing as this will prevent a quick repeat jump or acceleration away from the landing.

DRILL ARM MECHANICS – MIRROR/PARTNER

Aim
To perfect the correct arm technique for running in soccer.

Area/equipment
A large mirror.

For partner drill – work with a partner.

Description
The player stands in front of the mirror with his arms "ready" for sprinting, and performs short bursts of arm drives. Use the mirror as a feedback tool to perfect the technique.

For partner drill – the player stands with their partner behind them. The partner holds the palms of his hands in line with the player's elbows, fingers pointing upwards. The player fires the arms as if sprinting, so that the elbows "smack" into their partner's palms.

Key teaching points
- The arms should not move across the body
- Keep the elbows at 90°
- The hands and shoulders should be relaxed
- The inside of the wrists should brush against the pockets
- Ensure that the player performs a full ROM – the hands should move from the buttock cheeks to the chest or head

Sets and reps
3 sets of 16 reps, with 1 minute's recovery between each set.

Variations/progressions
Use light hand weights for the first 2 sets, controlling the movement carefully on the upswing; perform the last set without.

DRILL ARM MECHANICS – BUTTOCK BOUNCES

Aim
To develop explosive arm drive.

Area/equipment
Suitable ground surface.

Description
The player sits on the floor with his legs straight out in front of him. The arms are fired rapidly in short bursts. The power generated should be great enough to raise his buttocks off the floor in a bouncing manner.

Key teaching points
- The arms should not move across the body
- The elbows should be at 90°
- Keep the hands and shoulders relaxed
- The inside of the wrists should brush against the pockets
- ROM – the hands should move from the buttock cheek to the chest or head
- Encourage power in the movement

Sets and reps
3 sets of 6 reps. Each rep is 6–8 explosive arm drives with 1 minute's recovery between each set.

Variations/progressions
Use light hand weights for the first 2 sets, controlling the movement carefully on the upswing; perform the last set without.

DRILL RUNNING FORM – DEAD-LEG RUN

Aim
To develop a quick knee-lift and the positive foot placement required for effective sprinting.

Area/equipment
Indoor or outdoor area. Using hurdles, cones or sticks, place approximately 8 obstacles in a straight line at 2-foot intervals. Place a cone 1 yard from each end of the line to mark a start and finish.

Description
The player must keep the outside leg straight in a "locked" position. The inside leg moves over the obstacles in a "cycle"-type motion, while the outside leg swings along just above the ground (*see* fig. 2.1).

Key teaching points
- Bring the knee of the inside leg up to just below 90°
- Point the toe upwards
- Bring the inside leg back down quickly between the hurdles
- Increase the speed when the technique has been mastered
- Maintain correct arm mechanics
- Maintain an upright posture
- Keep the hips square and stand tall

Sets and reps
1 set of 6 reps, 3 leading off the left leg and 3 leading off the right leg.

Variations/progressions
Use light hand weights – accelerate off the end of the last obstacle and drop the hand weights during this acceleration phase.

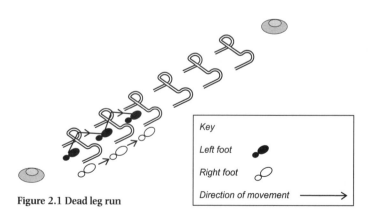

Key	
Left foot	
Right foot	
Direction of movement	⟶

Figure 2.1 Dead leg run

DRILL — RUNNING FORM – PRE-TURN

Aim
To educate and prepare the hips, legs and feet for effective and quick turning without fully committing the whole body.

Area/equipment
Indoor or outdoor area. Using hurdles, cones or sticks, place approximately 8 obstacles in a straight line at 2-foot intervals. Place a cone 1 yard from each end of the line to mark a start and finish.

Description
The player moves sideways along the line of obstacles, just behind them – i.e not traveling over them (*see* fig. 2.2). The back leg (following leg) is brought over the hurdle to a position slightly in front of the body, so that the heel is in line with the toe of the leading foot. As the back foot is planted, the leading foot moves away. Repeat the drill leading with the opposite leg.

Key teaching points
■ Stand tall and do not sink into the hips
■ Do not allow the feet to cross over
■ Keep the feet shoulder-width apart as much as possible
■ The knee-lift should be no greater than 45°
■ Maintain correct arm mechanics
■ Maintain an upright posture
■ Keep the hips and shoulders square

Sets and reps
1 set of 6 reps, 3 leading with the left shoulder and 3 leading with the right shoulder.

Variations/progressions
Use light hand weights – at the end of the obstacles, turn and accelerate 5 yards. Drop the weights halfway through the acceleration phase.

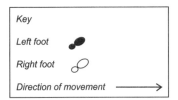

Key

Left foot

Right foot

Direction of movement

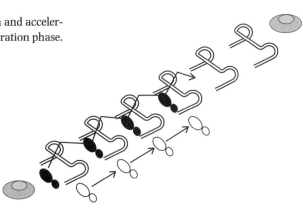

Figure 2.2 Pre-turn

DRILL RUNNING FORM – LEADING LEG RUN

Aim

To develop quick, efficient steps and running technique.

Area/equipment

Indoor or outdoor area. Using hurdles, cones or sticks, place approximately 8 obstacles in a straight line at 2-foot intervals. Place a cone 1 yard from each end of the line to mark a start and finish.

Description

The player runs down the line of obstacles, crossing over each one with the same lead leg (*see* fig. 2.3). The aim is to just clear the obstacles. Repeat the drill using the opposite leg as the lead.

Key teaching points

- The knee lift should be no more than 45°
- Use short, sharp steps
- Maintain strong arm mechanics
- Maintain an upright posture: stand tall and do not sink into the hips

Sets and reps

1 set of 6 reps, 3 leading with the left leg and 3 leading with the right leg.

Variations/progressions

This is great for changing direction after running in a straight line. Place 3 cones at the end of the obstacles and at different angles, approximately 2–3 yards away. On leaving the last obstacle, the player sprints out to the cone nominated by the coach.

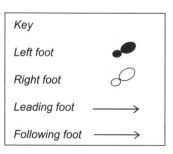

Key

Left foot

Right foot

Leading foot ⟶

Following foot ⟶

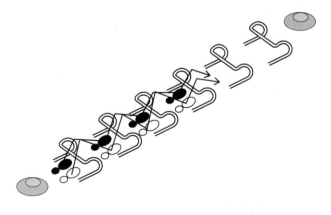

Figure 2.3 Left and right leg lead

DRILL   *RUNNING FORM – LATERAL STEPPING*

Aim
To develop efficient and economical lateral steps.

Area/equipment
Indoor or outdoor area. Using hurdles, cones or sticks, place approximately 8 obstacles in a straight line at 2-foot intervals. Place a cone 1 yard from each end of the line to mark a start and finish.

Description
The player steps over each obstacle while moving sideways (*see* fig. 2.4).

Key teaching points
■ Bring the knee up to just below 45°
■ Do not skip sideways – step!
■ Push off from the back foot
■ Do not pull with the lead foot
■ Maintain correct arm mechanics
■ Maintain an upright posture
■ Keep the hips square
■ Do not sink into the hips

Sets and reps
1 set of 6 reps, 3 leading with the left shoulder and 3 leading with the right shoulder.

Variations/progressions
Use light hand weights – accelerate off the end of the last obstacle and drop the hand weights during this acceleration phase.

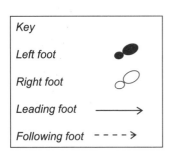

Key

Left foot

Right foot

Leading foot   ⟶

Following foot   - - - -›

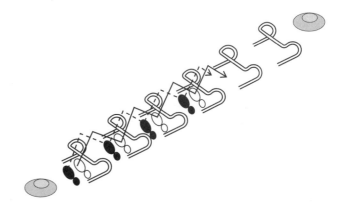

Figure 2.4 Lateral step

DRILL RUNNING FORM – 1-2-3 LIFT

Aim
To develop an efficient leg cycle, rhythm, power and foot placement.

Area/equipment
Indoor or outdoor area – 30–40 yards long.

Description
The player moves in a straight line, and after every third step the leg is brought up in an explosive action to 90°. Continue the drill along the length prescribed working the same leg, and then repeat the drill leading with the opposite leg.

Key teaching points
- Keep the hips square
- Work off the balls of the feet
- Try to develop and maintain a rhythm
- Keep eyes and head up and look ahead
- Maintain correct arm mechanics
- Maintain an upright posture
- Keep the hips square

Sets and reps
1 set of 6 reps, 3 leading with the left leg and 3 leading with the right leg.

Variations/progressions
- Alternate the lead leg during a repetition.
- Vary the lift sequence, e.g. 1-2-3-4-lift, etc.

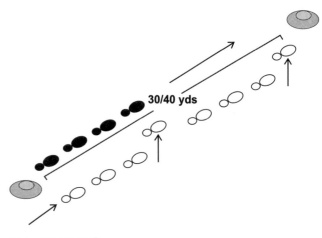

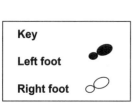

| **Key** |
| **Left foot** |
| **Right foot** |

Figure 2.5 1-2-3 Lift

DRILL   JUMPING – TWO-FOOTED SINGLES

Aim
To develop jumping technique, power, speed and control.

Area/equipment
Indoor or outdoor area. Ensure that the surface is clear of any obstacles. Use 7" or 12" hurdles.

Description
The player jumps over a single hurdle and on landing, walks back to the start point to repeat the drill, this will allow suitable time for recovery.

Key teaching points
■ Maintain good arm mechanics
■ Do not sink into the hips at the take-off and landing phases
■ Land on the balls of the feet
■ Do not fall back on to the heels

Sets and reps
2 sets of 8 reps, with 1 minute's recovery between each set.

Variations/progressions
■ Single jumps over the hurdle and back (*see* fig. 2.6(a)).
■ Single jumps over the hurdle with a 180° twist (NB: practice twisting to both sides – *see* fig. 2.6(b)).
■ Lateral single jumps – use both sides to jump off (*see* photo and fig. 2.6(c)).

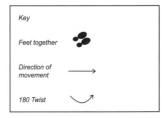

Key

Feet together

Direction of movement

180 Twist

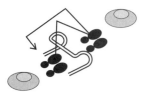

Figure 2.6(a) Two-footed single jump

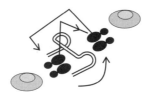

Figure 2.6(b) Two-footed single jump with 180° twist

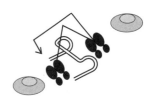

Figure 2.6(c) Two-footed lateral single jump

DRILL JUMPING – MULTIPLE JUMPS

Aim
To develop maximum control while taking off and landing. To develop controlled directional power.

Area/equipment
Indoor or outdoor area. Place 6–8 hurdles – either 7" or 12" high – at 2-foot intervals in a straight line.

Description
The player jumps over each hurdle in quick succession until all hurdles have been cleared (*see* fig. 2.7(a)). Walk back to the start and repeat the drill.

Key teaching points
- Use quick, rhythmic arm mechanics
- Do not sink into the hips at the take-off and landing phases
- Land and take off from the balls of the feet
- Stand tall and look straight ahead
- Maintain control
- Gradually build up the speed

Sets and reps
2 sets of 6 reps, with 1 minute's recovery between each set.

Variations/progressions
- Lateral jumps (*see* fig. 2.7(b)).
- Jumps with a 180° twist (*see* fig. 2.7(c)). NB: practice twisting to both sides.
- Hop over the hurdles, balance and then repeat (*see* fig. 2.7(d)).
- Use light hand weights – for the last rep of each of these sets, perform the drill without the weights as a contrast.

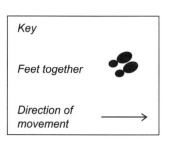

Key

Feet together

Direction of movement

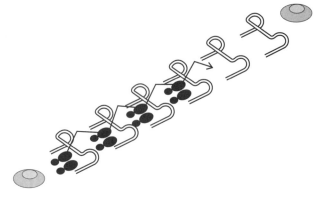

Figure 2.7(a) Multiple jumps

JUMPING – MULTIPLE JUMPS

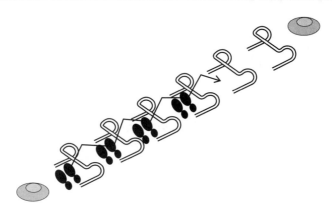

Figure 2.7(b) Lateral jumps

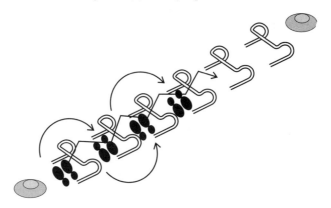

Figure 2.7(c) Jump with 180° twist

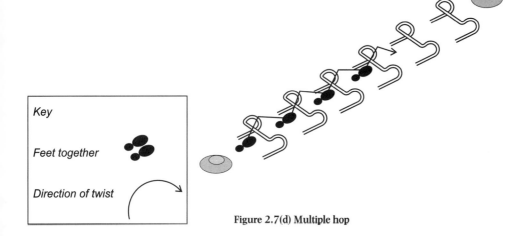

Key

Feet together

Direction of twist

Figure 2.7(d) Multiple hop

DRILL
RUNNING FORM –
STRIDE FREQUENCY AND STRIDE LENGTH

Aim
To practice the transfer from the acceleration phase to an increase in stride frequency and length required when running. To develop an efficient leg cycle, rhythm, power and foot placement.

Area/equipment
Indoor or outdoor area, 40–60 yards long. 12 colored sticks or canes, 4 feet in length, are placed flat on the ground at intervals of 5–6 feet (the intervals will be determined by the size and age of the group you are working with).

Description
Starting 20 yards away from the first stick, the player accelerates towards the stick and on reaching it steps just over it. The player then continues with a measured stride frequency and length as dictated by the sticks. On leaving the last stick or cane the player gradually decelerates. Return to the start and repeat the drill.

Key teaching points
- Do not over-stride
- Work off the balls of the feet
- Try to develop and maintain a rhythm
- Keep eyes/head up as if looking over a fence
- Maintain correct mechanics
- Maintain an upright posture
- Stay focused

Sets and reps
1 set of 4 reps.

Variations/progressions
- Set up the stride frequency sticks as shown in figure 2.8. The sticks now control the acceleration and deceleration phases.
- Add a change of direction during the deceleration phase.

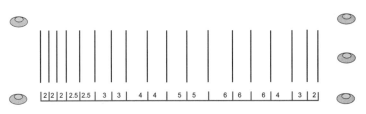

Figure 2.8 Stride frequency/length stick grid

DRILL *RUNNING FORM – WITH A BALL*

Aim
To maintain good mechanics when faced with soccer-specific stresses with the inclusion of a ball. To improve decision-making ability.

Area/equipment
Indoor or outdoor area. Place 8 hurdles in a straight line at 2-foot intervals. Place a cone at each end approximately 2 yards from the first and last cones respectively.

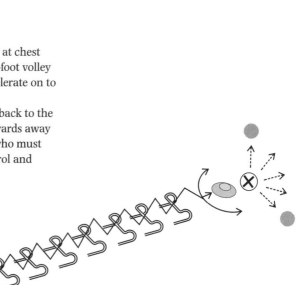

Description
The coach stands at the end cone with the ball. The player performs any one of the above mechanics drills through the hurdles (e.g. simple dead-leg run), and on clearing the final hurdle accelerates on to the ball that has been fed in at various angles by the coach (*see* fig. 2.9(a)).

Key teaching points
■ Maintain correct mechanics
■ Stay focused by looking ahead
■ Fire the arms explosively when accelerating to the ball

Sets and reps
3 sets of 6 reps. NB: the sets should be made up of various mechanics drills.

Variations/progressions
■ On clearing the final hurdle, the ball is fed to the player at chest height. The player controls the ball and executes a side-foot volley to the coach, who lays the ball off for the player to accelerate on to (*see* fig. 2.9(b)).
■ The player performs lateral mechanics drills with their back to the coach; the coach also works laterally approximately 2 yards away from the player. The coach feeds the ball to the player who must then turn to the left or right as instructed, gather, control and return the ball (*see* fig. 2.9(c) and photo on page 44).

Key	
Direction of run	⟶
Coach	Ⓧ
Player	✗
Ball	●
Direction of ball	- - - - - ➔

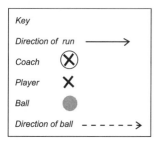

Figure 2.9(a) Running mechanics with ball

RUNNING FORM – WITH A BALL contd.

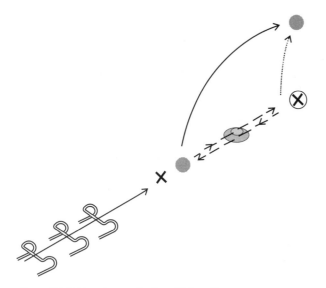

Figure 2.9(b) Running mechanics with lay-off

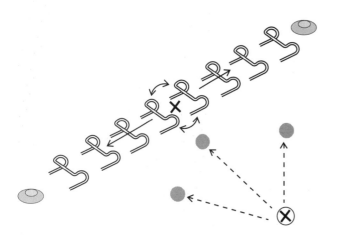

Figure 2.9(c) Running lateral mechanics with turn

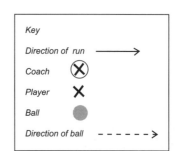

Key	
Direction of run	⟶
Coach	⊗
Player	✕
Ball	●
Direction of ball	– – – ⟶

DRILL   *RUNNING FORM – HURDLE MIRROR DRILLS*

Aim
To improve the performance of mechanics under pressure. To improve random agility.

Area/equipment
Indoor or outdoor area. Mark out a grid of 2 lines of 8 hurdles, with 2 feet between each hurdle and about 2 yards between each line of hurdles.

Description
Players face each other while performing mechanics drills up and down the lines of hurdles. One player initiates the movements while their partner attempts to mirror them (*see* fig. 2.10(a)). Players can perform both lateral and linear mirror drills.

Key teaching points
- Stay focused on your partner
- The player mirroring should try to anticipate the lead player's movements
- Maintain correct arm mechanics

Sets and reps
Each player performs 3 sets of 30-second work periods. There should be 30 seconds' recovery between each work period.

Variations/progressions
- First-to-the-ball drill – as above, except a ball is placed between the 2 lines of hurdles. The proactive partner commences the drill as normal then accelerates to the ball, collects it and dribbles to an end cone. The reactive player attempts to beat the proactive player to the ball (*see* fig. 2.10(b)).
- Lateral drills performed as above – players work in pairs with only 2 hurdles per player. These are great for improving short-stepping, lateral marking skills (*see* fig. 2.10(c)).

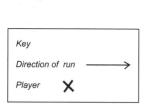

Key	
Direction of run	⟶
Player	**X**

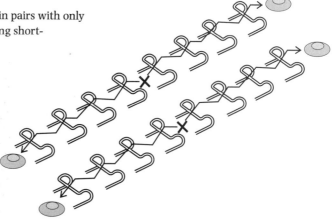

Figure 2.10(a) Mirror drills with hurdles

MIRROR DRILLS WITH HURDLES contd.

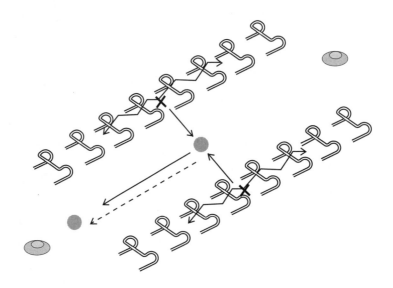

Figure 2.10(b) First-to-the-ball mirror drills

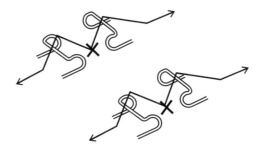

Figure 2.10(c) Short-stepping mirror drills

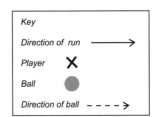

DRILL RUNNING FORM – COMPLEX MECHANICS

Aim
To prevent players resorting to "bad" form, particularly when under pressure. To challenge players by placing them in game-like pressure situations, and to maintain good running form even in the most difficult and demanding of situations.

Area/equipment
Indoor or outdoor area. Place 4 hurdles in a straight line with 2 feet between each hurdle. The next 4 hurdles are set slightly to one side and the final 4 hurdles are placed back in line with the original set (*see* fig. 2.11(a) overleaf).

Description
The player performs a dead-leg run (*see* page 34) over the hurdles, with the dead leg changing over the 4 center hurdles. Return to the start by performing the drill over the hurdles in the opposite direction.

Key teaching points
- Maintain correct arm mechanics
- Work off the balls of the feet
- Try to develop and maintain a rhythm
- Keep eyes/head up and look forwards
- Maintain an upright posture
- Keep the hips square

Sets and reps
4 sets of 4 reps.

Variations/progressions
Perform the drill laterally, moving both forwards and backwards to cross the center 4 hurdles (*see* fig. 2.11(b) overleaf).

COMPLEX MECHANICS contd.

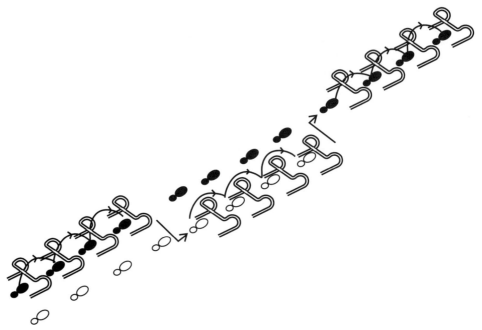

Figure 2.11(a) Complex mechanic drills

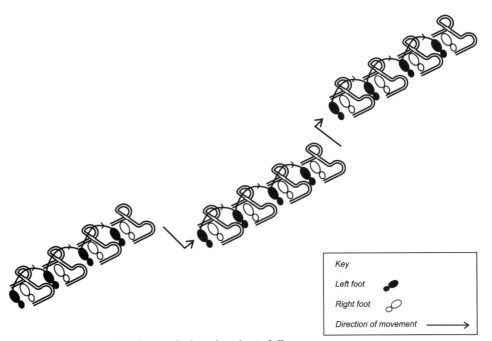

Figure 2.11(b) Complex lateral mechanic drills

CHAPTER 3 INNERVATION

FAST FEET, AGILITY AND CONTROL FOR SOCCER

This is the transition stage from the warm-up and mechanics to periods of high-intensity work that activates the neural pathways – in other words, getting the nerves to fire the muscles as quickly as possible. Using the Fast Foot Ladder, dance-like patterns such as twists, jumps and turns are all introduced. Soccer-specific footwork drills that require speed, co-ordination and agility such as side-step shuffles are practiced explosively with and without the ball. The key here is to speed up the running techniques without compromising the quality of the mechanics.

The innervation drills in this chapter progress from simple footwork patterns to complex, soccer-specific drills.

DRILL FAST FOOT LADDER – SINGLE RUNS

Aim
To develop fast feet with control, precision and power.

Area/equipment
Indoor or outdoor area – Fast Foot Ladder. Ensure that this is the correct ladder for the type of surface being used.

Description
The player covers the length of the ladder by placing one foot in each ladder space (*see* fig. 3.1(a)). Return to the start by jogging back on the outside of the ladder.

Key teaching points
- Maintain correct running form/mechanics
- Start slowly and gradually increase the speed
- Maintain an upright posture
- Stress that quality, not quantity, is important

Sets and Reps
3 sets of 4 reps, with 1 minute's recovery between each set.

Variations/progressions
- Single lateral step – as above but performed laterally (*see* fig. 3.1(b)).
- In-and-out – moving sideways along the ladder, stepping into and out of each ladder space (i.e. both feet in and both feet out, *see* fig. 3.1(c)).
- "Icky shuffle" – side-stepping movement into and out of each ladder space whilst moving forwards (*see* fig. 3.1(d)).
- Double run – perform as single run above but with both feet in each ladder space (*see* fig. 3.1(e)).
- Hopscotch – perform as double run above but with both feet outside the ladder on alternate spaces (*see* fig. 3.1(f)).
- Single space jumps – two footed jumps into and out of each ladder space (*see* fig. 3.1(g)).

Figure 3.1(a) Single runs

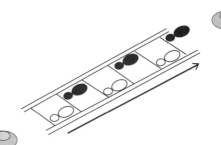

Figure 3.1(b) Single lateral step

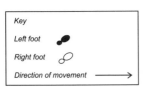

Key

Left foot

Right foot

Direction of movement ⟶

FAST FOOT LADDER – SINGLE RUNS cont.

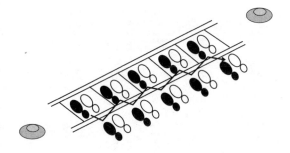

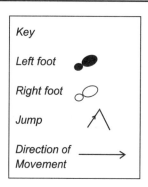

Key

Left foot

Right foot

Jump

Direction of Movement

Figure 3.1(c) In-and-out

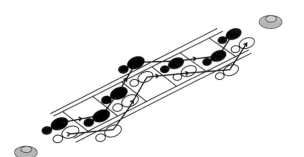

Figure 3.1(d) "Icky shuffle"

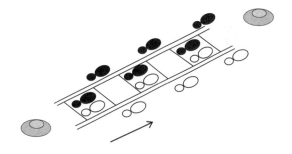

Figure 3.1(f) Hopscotch

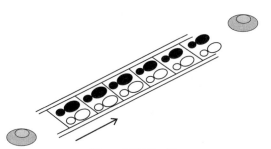

Figure 3.1(e) Double run

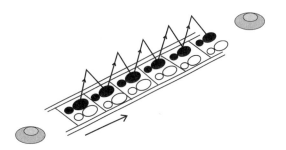

Figure 3.1(g) Single-space jumps

DRILL FAST FOOT LADDER – "T" FORMATION

Aim
To develop speed of acceleration when pressing the opposition. To develop controlled lateral cross-cover and defensive backwards jockeying movements.

Area/equipment
Indoor or outdoor area – place 2 ladders in a "T" formation with 3 cones placed at the end of each ladder.

Description
The player accelerates down the ladder using single steps. On reaching the ladder and crossing the end, the player moves laterally either left or right using short lateral steps. On coming out of the ladder the player then jockeys backwards toward the start line.

Key teaching points
■ Maintain correct running form/mechanics
■ Encourage strong arm drive when transferring from linear to lateral steps
■ When jockeying backwards, keep the head and eyes up

Sets and reps
3 sets of 4 reps (2 moving to the left and 2 moving to the right), with 1 minute's recovery between each set.

Variations/progressions
■ Start with a lateral run, and upon reaching the end ladder, accelerate in a straight line forwards down the ladder.
■ Mix and match previous quick-foot ladder drills (*see* page 50–51).

Key

Direction of movement ⟶

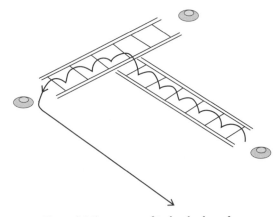

Figure 3.2 Up, across and jockey backwards

DRILL *FAST FOOT LADDER – CROSSOVER*

Aim
To develop speed, agility and change of direction in a more soccer-specific, "crowded" area. To improve reaction time, peripheral vision and timing.

Area/equipment
Large indoor or outdoor area – place 4 ladders in a cross formation, leaving a clear center space of approximately 3 square yards. Place a cone 1 yard from the start of each ladder.

Description
Split the squad into 4 equal groups and locate them at the start of each ladder (A, B, C and D on fig. 3.3(a)). Players accelerate down the ladder, performing a single-step drill. On reaching the end of the ladder, players accelerate across the center square and onwards to join the end of the line at the start of the ladder opposite them. Do not travel down this ladder!

Key teaching points
- Maintain correct running form/mechanics
- Keep the head and eyes up and be aware of other players, particularly around the center area

Sets and reps
3 sets of 6 reps, with 1 minute's recovery between each set.

Variations/progressions
- At the end of the first ladder, side-step to the right or left and single-step down the appropriate adjacent ladder (*see* fig. 3.3(b)).
- Vary the quick-foot ladder drills performed down the first ladder.
- Include a 360° turn in the center square. This is great for positional awareness.

Key	
Direction of movement	⟶

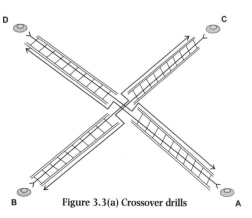

Figure 3.3(a) Crossover drills

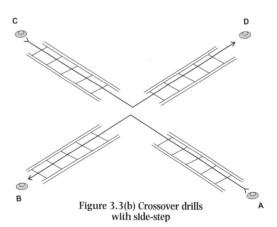

Figure 3.3(b) Crossover drills with side-step

DRILL   FAST FOOT LADDER – WITH A BALL

Aim

To develop fast feet, speed and agility while incorporating game-specific ball control.

Area/equipment

Large indoor or outdoor area. Place a Fast Foot Ladder with a cone at each end, approximately 1 yard away.

Description

One player performs fast-foot drills down the ladder (see pages 50–51), either laterally or linearly, while a second player, standing 2 yards away from the ladder in a central position, feeds the ball into him at different heights – requiring the first player to perform either a foot, chest or head skill to control and return the ball.

Key teaching points

- Concentrate on good footwork patterns
- Ensure that correct technical skills are used when controlling and returning the ball
- Ensure that the player performing the drill returns to correct running form/mechanics having returned the ball

Sets and reps

3 sets of 6 reps, with 1 minute's recovery between each set.

Variations/progressions

Vary the quick-foot ladder drills performed by the player (*see* pages 50–51).

Key	
Direction of run	⟶
Coach	Ⓧ
Player	✕
Ball	●
Direction of ball	- - - - ➤

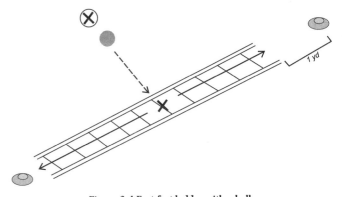

Figure 3.4 Fast-feet ladder with a ball

DRILL | *FAST FOOT LADDER – WITH PASSING*

Aim

To develop fast feet and agility while incorporating soccer-specific ball control and passing combination drills.

Area/equipment

Large indoor or outdoor area. Place two ladders in an upside-down "L" pattern, with two more mirroring these, approximately 2 yards away. Place cones at the start and end of each "L" (1 yard away). Place another 2 cones 15 yards away and 1 yard apart in line with the center space. At the end of one ladder, place a ball.

Description

Two players start with linear fast-foot drills, then transfer to lateral drills as the ladders dictate. Player 1 accelerates on to the ball and dribbles for 2 yards before passing the ball on for Player 2 to move on to. On receiving the ball Player 2 takes just one or two touches before passing the ball back to Player 1, who shoots the ball through the cones. The players jog back to the start where they swap roles.

Key teaching points

- Maintain correct running form/mechanics
- Ensure that correct technical skills are used when the players are on the ball
- Encourage the players to use clear communication – both visual and audio

Sets and reps

3 sets of 6 reps, with 1 minute's recovery between each set (i.e. 3 reps as player 1 and 3 reps as player 2).

Variations/progressions

Vary the quick-foot ladder drills performed linearly and laterally by the players (*see* pages 50–51).

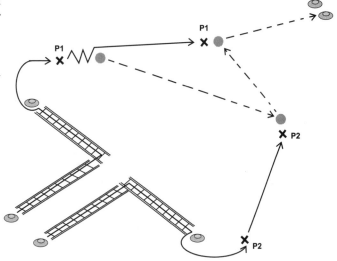

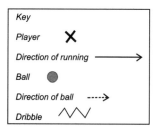

Key	
Player	**X**
Direction of running	——→
Ball	●
Direction of ball	---→
Dribble	∧∧∨

Figure 3.5 Fast feet ladder with passing drill

DRILL   FAST FOOT LADDER "IPSWICH TOWN GRID"

Aim

To develop fast feet, agility and control in a restricted area while under pressure from other players.

Area/equipment

Large indoor or outdoor area – place 4 ladders side-by-side.

Description

Working in pairs, players perform fast-foot drills while covering the length of the outside ladders (*see* fig. 3.6(a)). On the coach's signal the players move to the inside ladders, thus working side-by-side. On reaching the end they jog back to the start line.

Key teaching points

- Maintain correct running form/mechanics
- Encourage the players to push and nudge each other to simulate the close-marking situations that occur in a game
- If players are "knocked" off balance, ensure they re-assert the correct arm mechanics as soon as possible

Sets and reps

3 sets of 4 reps, with 1 minute's recovery between each set.

Variations/progressions

- Start players on the central ladders and work them out and back in.
- Start players on ladders next to each other on either the left or right of the grid, and work them across the 4 ladders (*see* fig. 3.6(b)).

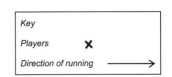

Key

Players   **X**

Direction of running ———→

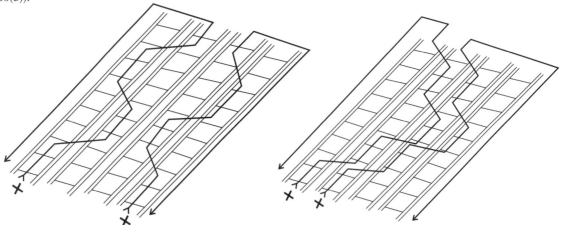

Figure 3.6(a) "Ipswich Town Grid"   Figure 3.6(b) "Ipswich Town Grid" progression

DRILL · FAST FOOT LADDER GIANT CROSSOVER

Aim

To develop fast feet, speed, agility, co-ordination and visual reaction skills both with and without the ball.

Area/equipment

Large indoor or outdoor area. Place 4 ladders in a cross formation with 25 yards between the ladders in the center area. Place a ball at the end of one ladder and another at the end of an adjacent ladder.

Description

Split the squad into 4 equal groups and locate them at the start of each ladder (*see* fig. 3.7). Players accelerate down the ladder, performing fast-foot drills (*see* pages 50–51). Two players will have a ball at the end of their respective ladders; they dribble the ball across the center area and pass it to the oncoming player, who receives and controls the ball before passing it on to the next oncoming player. Having passed the ball the player runs to the start of the line on the opposite side of the cross. Do not travel down this ladder!

Key teaching points

- This should be a continuous drill
- Maintain correct running form/mechanics
- Ensure that correct technical skills are used when players are on the ball
- Encourage players to use clear communication

Sets and reps

3 sets of 6 reps, with 1 minute's recovery between each set.

Variations/progressions

- Vary the passing drills used in the center area.
- Vary the amount of control allowed, e.g. one touch, two touches, etc.

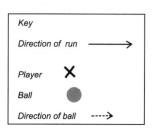

Key

Direction of run ⟶

Player ✗

Ball ●

Direction of ball ----→

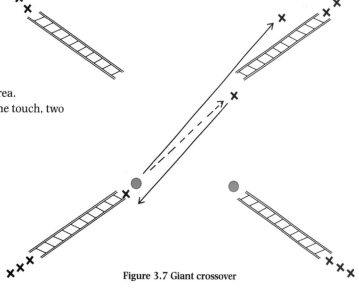

Figure 3.7 Giant crossover

DRILL   *FAST FOOT LADDER – LONG PASS*

Aim

To develop fast feet, speed, agility and acceleration while focusing on getting into position early to receive a long pass. To develop accurate passing over long distances.

Area/equipment

Large indoor or outdoor area, with 4 ladders. Place 2 ladders next to each other, 10 yards apart. The other 2 ladders should be placed in the same formation, 40–50 yards away. Place a ball at the end of each of the first 2 ladders.

Description

Split the squad into 4 equal groups and locate them at the ends of each ladder so all players are facing the center space. Players perform nominated fast-foot drills down the ladders (*see* pages 50–51). Two players collect the balls at the ends of their ladders and make long, straight passes to the players coming down the opposite ladders (*see* fig. 3.8(a)). On completing the passes the players jockey backwards to their start positions.

Key teaching points

- Maintain correct running form/mechanics
- Ensure that correct technical skills are used when players are on the ball
- The timing of the player who is to receive the ball is crucial – they should receive the ball just as they leave the ladder to enter the center space
- The player receiving the ball should do so on the move, not standing still

Sets and reps

3 sets of 6 reps, with 1 minute's recovery between each set.

Variations/progressions

- Make the long pass a diagonal pass to the oncoming player on the ladder next door.
- For sprint endurance conditioning, make the players accelerate across the center space (*see* fig. 3.8(b)) to join the start of the ladder diagonally opposite them.

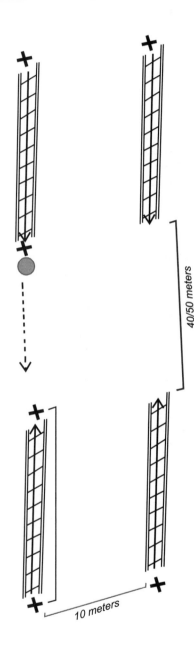

Figure 3.8(a) Fast-feet long pass

FAST FOOT LADDER – LONG PASS

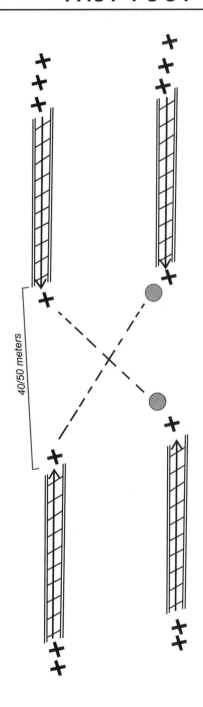

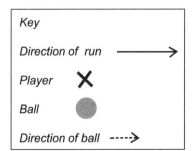

Key

Direction of run →

Player ✗

Ball ●

Direction of ball ----->

Figure 3.8(b) Fast-feet long diagonal pass

DRILL | LINE DRILLS

Aim
To develop quickness of the feet.

Area/equipment
Indoor or outdoor area – use any line marked on the ground surface.

Description
The player performs single split steps over the line and back – right foot forward, left foot back, then right foot back, left foot forward (*see* fig. 3.9(a)).

Key teaching points
- Maintain good arm mechanics
- Maintain an upright posture
- Maintain a strong core
- Try to develop a rhythm
- Keep the head and eyes up

Sets and reps
3 sets of 20 reps, with 1 minute's recovery between each set.

Variations/progressions
- Two-footed jumps over the line and back (*see* fig. 3.9(b)).
- Stand astride the line and bring the feet in to touch the line before sending them back out again. Perform the drill as quickly as possible (*see* fig. 3.9(c)).
- Two-footed side jumps over the line and back (*see* fig. 3.9(d)).
- Two-footed side jumps with a 180° twist in the air over the line and back (*see* fig. 3.9(e)).
- Complex variation – introduce the ball either at the end of the drill so that the player explodes on to it, or during the drill so that the player passes it back before continuing with the drill.

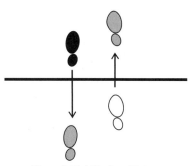

Figure 3.9(a) Single split steps

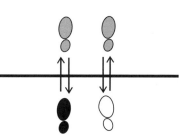

Figure 3.9(b) Two-footed jumps

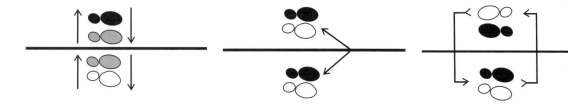

Figure 3.9(c) Astride jumps   Figure 3.9(d) Two-footed side jumps over and back   Figure 3.9(e) Two-footed side jumps with 180° twist

DRILL | *QUICK BOX STEPS*

Aim
To develop explosive power and control. NB: the emphasis is on speed.

Area/equipment
Indoor or outdoor area – a bench, aerobics step or suitable strong box with a non-slip surface, approximately 12" in height.

Description
The player performs an alternating split step jump on the box – i.e. one foot on the box and one on the floor (*see* fig. 3.10(a)).

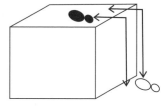

Figure 3.10(a) Split step jump

Key teaching points
- Practice the drill slowly first to perfect balance and the foot placement, then build up speed
- Focus on good arm drive
- Maintain an upright posture
- Maintain a strong core
- Keep the head and eyes up
- Work off the balls of the feet
- Work at a high intensity and technique is perfected
- Try to develop a rhythm

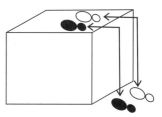

Figure 3.10(b) Two-footed jumps

Sets and reps
3 sets of 20 reps, with 1 minute's recovery between each set.

Variations/progressions
- Two-footed jumps on to and off of the box (*see* fig. 3.10(b)).
- Two-footed side jumps on to and off of the box (lead with the left shoulder for 10 reps and then the right shoulder for 10 reps) (*see* fig. 3.10(c)).
- Straddle jumps on to and off of the box (*see* fig. 3.10(d)).
- Single-footed hops on and off of the box (lead with the left foot for 10 reps and then the right foot for 10 reps) (*see* fig. 3.10(e)).

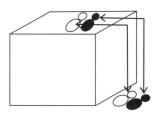

Figure 3.10(c) Two-footed side jumps

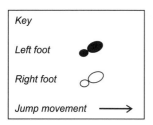

Key

Left foot

Right foot

Jump movement ⟶

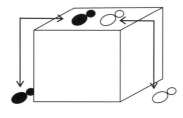

Figure 3.10(d) Straddle jumps

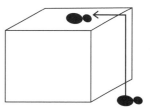

Figure 3.10(e) Single-footed hops

CHAPTER 4 ACCUMULATION OF POTENTIAL

THE SAQ SOCCER CIRCUIT

This is the part of the continuum where we bring together those areas of work already practiced. Many of the mechanics and fast-foot drills are specific to developing a particular skill. In soccer, though, the skills are not isolated but clustered. An example of this is when a player needs to run mechanically well for 30 yards, decelerate, move with fast feet to change direction, jump, turn, side-step and then stop and assess the situation. All this may occur over a varying period of time.

Using ladders, hurdles, cones and poles, etc., soccer-specific circuits can be used to develop programmed agility as well as conditioning the player for this type of high-intensity work.

> Do not use this phase to fatigue the players but to challenge them with a variety of skills. Ensure that a maximum recovery period is implemented between sets and reps.

DRILL T-RUNS

Aim
To develop soccer-specific speed and agility.

Area/equipment
Indoor or outdoor area. Place 4 poles or cones 5 yards apart in a "T" formation (*see* fig. 4.1(a)).

Description
The player starts on the left-hand side of the first pole and accelerates to the pole directly ahead. He then passes around this pole and turns to his right before accelerating on to the end pole. The player then runs around the end pole and returns to the middle pole before finishing on the opposite side at the start position (*see* fig. 4.1(b)). Repeat the drill by starting on the right of the first pole and turning to the left at the middle pole.

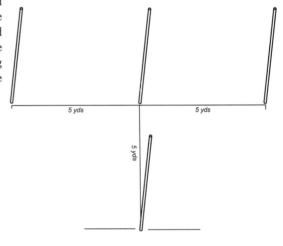

Figure 4.1(a) T-run grid

Key teaching points
- Maintain correct running form/mechanics
- Work on shortening the steps used in the turn
- Focus on increasing the speed of the arm drive when coming out of the turns
- Ensure that players work their weak sides – most players will have a preferred turning side

Sets and reps
3 sets of 5 reps, with a 30-second recovery between each rep and 1 minute's recovery between each set.

Variations/progressions
The coach stands at the center cone. The player accelerates towards the coach, who provides a signal – verbal or visual – to dictate which way the player turns.

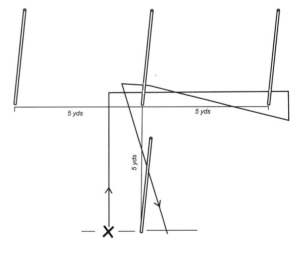

Figure 4.1(b) T-run right

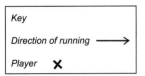

Key

Direction of running ⟶

Player ✗

DRILL   SWERVE-DEVELOPMENT RUNS

Aim
To develop fine-angle running at pace, as if trying to lose a close marker or create space to receive a ball.

Area/equipment
A large indoor or outdoor area. Set out 8–12 poles or cones in a "zig-zag" formation (*see* fig 4.2). The distance between the poles/cones should be 2–4 yards at varying angles (this will make the runs more realistic). The total length of the run will be 25–30 yards.

Description
The player accelerates from the first cone and swerves in and around all of the others before completing the course. The player gently jogs back to the starting cone before repeating the drill.

Key teaching points
- Maintain correct running form/mechanics
- Work on shortening the steps used in the turns
- Focus on increasing the speed of the arm drive when coming out of the turns
- Ensure that players take the tightest possible angles around the cones
- Keep the head and eyes up

Sets and reps
3 sets of 5 reps, with a 30-second recovery between each rep and 1 minute's recovery between each set.

Variations/progressions
Use light hand weights for the first 4 reps then perform the last rep without the weights as a contrast.

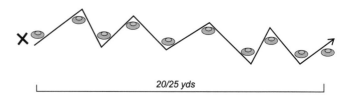

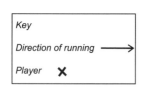

Key	
Direction of running	⟶
Player	**X**

20/25 yds

Figure 4.2 Swerve-development runs

DRILL ZIG-ZAG RUNS

Aim

To develop fast, controlled and angled lateral runs.

Area/equipment

Indoor or outdoor area. Mark out a grid using 10–12 poles or cones in 2 lines of 5–6. Stagger the poles/cones so that the line is in a zig-zag formation (*see* fig. 4.3(a)).

> Arm mechanics are as vital in lateral movements as they are in linear movements. Many players forget to use their arms when they are moving sideways.

Description

The player runs the zig-zag formation, staying on the inside of the cones/poles, and then walks back to the start before repeating the drill.

Key teaching points

- Maintain correct running form/mechanics
- Players must keep their hips facing the direction in which they are running
- Encourage players to use short steps
- Ensure that players do not skip
- Ensure that players use good arm mechanics

Sets and reps

3 sets of 6 reps, with a walk-back recovery between each rep and 1 minute's recovery between each set.

Variations/progressions

- Perform the drill backwards, using the jockeying movement.
- Players go *around* each cone rather than staying on the inside of them.
- Up-and-back – enter the grid sideways and move forwards to the first cone then backwards to the next, etc.
- Add a Fast Foot Ladder to the start and finish for acceleration and deceleration running (*see* fig. 4.3(b)).

Figure 4.3(a) Zig-zag run

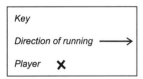

Key

Direction of running ———→

Player ✗

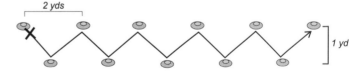

Figure 4.3(b) Ladder zig-zag run

DRILL SOCCER-SPECIFIC RUNS

Aim
To develop a creative range of soccer-specific running patterns likely to be encountered in games in order to enhance the players' skill base and keep them motivated and challenged.

Area/equipment
Half a soccer pitch with cones, hurdles, fast feet, ladders, poles and balls. These are all to be placed in a circuit within the area (*see* fig. 4.4).

Description
The players follow a circuit which will take them through ladders, get them stepping and jumping over hurdles, side-stepping through cones, running backwards, jumping, turning and performing ball skills. One circuit should take players 30–60 seconds to complete.

Key teaching points
■ Maintain correct running form/mechanics for all activities

Sets and reps
1 set of 6 reps with a varied recovery time between each rep, depending on the stage in the season.

Variations/progressions
The coach to use their imagination to add or subtract and vary the drills within the circuit. This will keep players motivated and challenged.

SOCCER-SPECIFIC RUNS

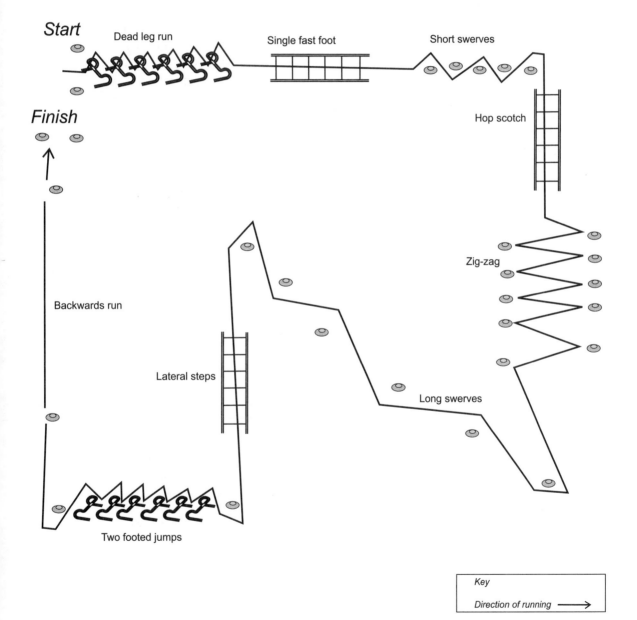

Figure 4.4 Soccer-specific runs

CHAPTER 5 EXPLOSION

3-STEP MULTI-DIRECTIONAL ACCELERATION FOR SOCCER

The exercises outlined in this chapter have been designed to boost response times and develop multi-directional, explosive movements.

Programmable and random agility is trained using resisted and assisted high-quality plyometrics. Plyometric exercises focus on the stretch shortening cycle of the muscles involved, an action that is a central part of soccer performance. Plyometric drills include drop jumps, hops, skips and bounds. Plyometrics can be fun and challenging and also add variety to training sessions. However, there is potential for injury with these exercises if they are not performed using the correct technique and at the correct point in the training session. Upper-body speed and power is also catered for with Jelly Ball workouts, effective in developing the type of strength required to hold off an opponent.

The crucial element in using explosive drills is the implementation of the "contrast phase." This simply means performing the drill without resistance for one or two reps immediately after performing them with resistance. These movements will naturally be more explosive and more easily remembered and reproduced over a period of time.

The key is to ensure that quality, not quantity, is the priority. Efforts must be carefully monitored.

> This is a time for fast action, not "tongue-hanging-out fatigue."

DRILL | *SEATED FORWARD GET-UP*

Aim
To develop multi-directional, explosive acceleration. To improve a player's ability to get up and accelerate all in one movement.

Area/equipment
Indoor or outdoor area of 20 square yards.

Description
The player sits on the floor, facing the direction in which he is going to run and with his legs straight out in front of him. On a signal from the coach, the player gets up as quickly as possible, accelerates for 10 yards and then slows down before jogging gently back to the start position.

Key teaching points
- Players should try to complete the drill in one smooth action
- Promote correct running form/mechanics
- Encourage the players to get into an upright position and to drive the arms as soon as possible
- Ensure that the initial steps are short and powerful
- Do not encourage over-striding

Sets and reps
3 sets of 5 reps, with a jog-back recovery between each rep and a 2-minute recovery between each set.

Variations/progressions
- Seated backward get-ups, turning to run forwards
- Seated sideways get-ups, turning to run forwards
- Laying get-ups from the front, back, left and right sides
- Kneeling get-ups
- Work in pairs and have get-up competitions chasing a ball
- Work in pairs with one player in front of the other and performing "tag" get-ups

DRILL FLEXI-CORD – BUGGY RUNS

Aim
To develop multi-directional, explosive acceleration.

Area/equipment
Indoor or outdoor area – place 3 cones in a line with 10 yards between each, and ensure that there is plenty of room for safe deceleration. 1 Viper Belt with a flexi-cord attached at both ends by 2 anchor points.

Description
Working in pairs, player 1 wears the belt while player 2 stands behind holding the flexi-cord with his hands looped in and over the flexi-cord (this is for safety purposes). Player 2 allows the flexi-cord to resist as player 1 accelerates forwards, then runs behind at a distance sufficient to maintain a constant resistance over the first 10 yards. Both players need to decelerate over the second 10 yards. Player 1 removes the belt after the required number of reps and completes a contrast run (*see* page 68) on his own. Repeat the drill but swap roles.

Key teaching points
- Player 1 must focus on correct running form/mechanics and explosive drive
- Player 2 works *with* player 1 not against, allowing the flexi-cord to provide the resistance

Sets and reps
1 set of 6 reps plus 1 contrast run, with 30 seconds' recovery between each rep and 3 minutes' recovery before the next drill.

Variations/progressions
- Lateral buggy run – player 1 accelerates laterally for the first 2 yards before turning to cover the remaining distance linearly.
- After the acceleration phase of the contrast run, the coach can introduce a ball for the player to run on to.

DRILL   FLEXI-CORD – OUT AND BACK

Aim
To develop short, explosive, angled accelerated runs – ideal for beating an opponent to the ball or into a space.

Area/equipment
Large indoor or outdoor area of 10 square yards would be ideal – 5 cones to be positioned as shown in the figure 5.1(a), 1 Viper Belt with a flexi-cord attached to only one anchor point on the belt, and a safety belt on the other end of the flexi-cord.

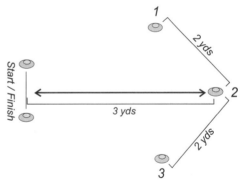

Description
Working in pairs, player 1 wears the Viper Belt. Player 2 stands directly behind player 1, holding the flexi-cord and wearing the safety belt. The flexi-cord should be taut prior to the drill commencing. Player 2 nominates a cone for player 1 to run out to, varying the calls between the 3 cones for the required number of repetitions. When player 1 arrives at the nominated cone a coach or a third player delivers a ball either to the head, chest or foot. This is controlled and passed back before player 1 returns to the start gate using short, sharp steps. Repeat for the prescribed number of reps, and finish with a contrast run before swapping roles.

Key teaching points
■ Focus on short, sharp, explosive steps and a fast powerful arm drive
■ Maintain correct running form/mechanics
■ Work off the balls of the feet
■ Use short steps while returning back to the start to help develop balance and control

Figure 5.1(a) Flexi-cord out-and-back grid

Sets and reps
3 sets of 6 reps plus 1 contrast run per set, with a 3-minute recovery between each set. For advanced players, depending on the time of the season, increase to 9 reps.

Variations/progressions
■ Perform the drill laterally.
■ Jockey backwards on the return phase with short, sharp steps.
■ Perform the drill backwards.

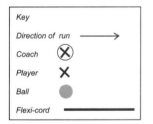

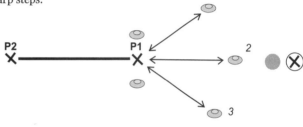

Figure 5.1(b) Flexi-cord out-and-back drill

DRILL   FLEXI-CORD – LATERAL BALL WORK

Aim

To develop explosive lateral movements with the ball at the feet.

Area/equipment

Indoor or outdoor area – 12 cones placed in a zig-zag formation (*see* fig. 5.2). 1 ball and 1 Viper Belt with a flexi-cord attached to only one anchor point on the belt, and a safety belt on the other end of the flexi-cord. Place 2 cones out to indicate the combined unstretched flexi-cord and safety belt distance (approximately 10–12 feet) to act as a guide for the partner.

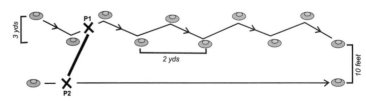

Description

Wearing the Viper Belt, player 1 runs a lateral zig-zag pattern between the cones, dribbling the ball at his feet. Player 2 works along the line between the 2 outside cones, slightly behind the partner; this ensures that the flexi-cord does not get in the way of the arm mechanics. Work up and back along the line of zig-zag cones. On completing the reps, player 1 removes the belt and performs a contrast run.

Key teaching points

- Use short, sharp steps. Do not bring the feet too close together or allow them to cross over
- Maintain correct lateral running form/mechanics
- No skipping
- Push off with the back foot – do not pull with the front foot

Sets and reps

3 sets of 6 reps plus 1 contrast run per set (work both the left and right sides – i.e. just turn the belt around on the player's waist), with a 3-minute recovery between each set.

Variations/progressions

Perform the drill backwards.

Key	
Direction of run	⟶
Player	✗
Flexi-cord	▬▬▬

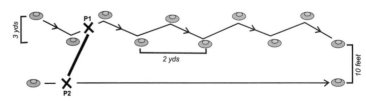

Figure 5.2 Flexi-cord – lateral ball work

DRILL FLEXI-CORD – VERTICAL POWER

Aim

To develop vertical take-off power for the production of more air time and height when jumping to head the ball, or to catch the ball as a goalkeeper.

Area/equipment

Indoor or outdoor area approximately 3–4 square yards. 1 Viper Belt with 2 flexi-cords and 1 ball.

Description

Working in groups of 4, 1 player wears the Viper Belt which has 2 flexi-cords attached – one attached on either side – by both of their ends (*see* photo). 2 players stand a yard away, one either side of the resisted player. They stand on the flexi-cords with their legs about 1 yard apart. The fourth player stands in front of the resisted player, holding the ball above his head. The resisted player jumps to head the ball before setting himself to repeat the drill.

Key teaching points

- Do not sink into the hips either before take-off or on landing
- Work off the balls of the feet
- On landing, regain balance and prepare before the next jump
- Maintain correct jumping form/mechanics for each rep

Sets and reps

3 sets of 8 reps plus 1 contrast jump, with 3 minutes' recovery between each set.

Variations/progressions

Quick jumps – i.e no setting between jumps. These are fast, repetitive jumps performed as quickly as possible.

DRILL   FLEXI-CORD – OVERSPEED

Aim
To develop lightning-quick acceleration.

Area/equipment
Indoor or outdoor area – 1 Viper Belt with a flexi-cord attached. 4 cones placed in a "T" formation with 3 yards between each cone (*see* fig. 5.3).

Description
Working in pairs, player 1 wears the Viper Belt and faces player 2. Player 2 has the safety belt around his waist – i.e the flexi-cord will go from belly button to belly button – and he holds the flexi-cord. Player 1 stands at cone A. Player 2 stands at cone B and walks backwards and away from player 1, therefore increasing the flexi-cord resistance. After stretching the flexi-cord for 4–5 yards, player 1 accelerates towards player 2 who then nominates either cone C or D – requiring player 1 to explosively change direction. Both players walk back to the start and repeat the drill.

Key teaching points
- Maintain and control correct running form/mechanics
- During the change of direction phase, shorten the steps and increase the rate of firing in the arms

Sets and reps
3 sets of 8 reps plus 1 contrast run, with 3 minutes' recovery between each set.

Variations/progressions
- Player 1 starts with a horizontal jump before accelerating away.
- Introduce the ball for the player to run on to after the change of direction phase.

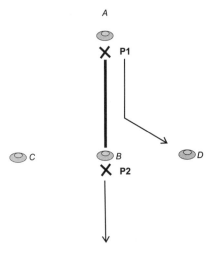

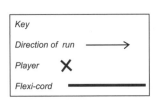

Figure 5.3 Flexi-cord – overspeed

DRILL   SIDE-STEPPER – LATERAL RUNS

Aim
To develop explosive, controlled lateral patterns of running.

Area/equipment
Indoor or outdoor area – 10–12 cones placed in a zig-zag pattern (*see* fig. 5.4) and a Side-Stepper.

Description
The player wearing the Side-Stepper covers the length of the grid by running a lateral zig-zag pattern between the cones. Just before arriving at the cone, he extends the last step to increase the level of resistance. On completing a run, he turns around and works back along the grid.

Key teaching points
■ Maintain correct lateral running form/mechanics
■ Do not sink into the hips when stepping off to change direction
■ During the directional change phase, increase arm speed to provide additional control

Sets and reps
3 sets of 6 reps plus 1 contrast run, with no recovery time between each rep and 3 minutes' recovery between each set.

Variations/progressions
■ Perform the drill backwards – i.e. using jockeying movement.
■ Include a ball.

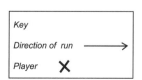

Key
Direction of run ⟶
Player X

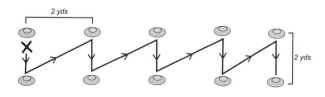

Figure 5.4 Side-stepper – resisted lateral runs

DRILL   SIDE-STEPPER JOCKEYING IN PAIRS

Aim
To develop man-to-man marking skills, with particular focus on defensive and attacking jockeying skills.

Area/equipment
Indoor or outdoor area – 6–8 cones. Mark out a channel approximately 20 yards long and 3 yards wide.

Description
Two players wearing Side-Steppers should face each other with approximately 2 yards between them. The attacking player moves from right to left in a jockeying pattern, while the defending player attempts to mirror the movements to prevent the attacking player from having too much space. In other words, the attacking player works in a forward direction and the defending player works backwards.

Key teaching points
- Use quick, low steps not high knees
- No skipping or jumping – one foot should be in contact with the floor at all times
- Try to keep the feet shoulder-width apart
- Use a powerful arm drive
- Do not sink into the hips

Sets and reps
3 sets of 4 reps plus contrast set of 2 reps, with a 30-second recovery between each rep and 2 minutes recovery between each set.

Variations/progressions
- Both players perform the drill laterally, with one player leading and the other trying to mirror their movements.
- Introduce a ball.

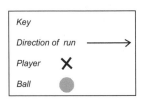

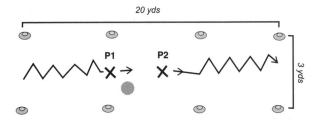

Figure 5.5 Side-Stepper resisted jockeying drills

DRILL *HAND-WEIGHT DROPS*

Aim
To develop explosive power, re-acceleration and, specifically, a powerful arm drive.

Area/equipment
Indoor or outdoor area – 3 cones, light hand weights (between 2–4 lb in weight). Place 1 cone down to represent the start, a second cone 15 yards away and the final cone 10 yards away from the second.

Description
The player holds the weights and accelerates to the second cone where he releases them, keeping a natural flow to the arm mechanics. He continues to accelerate to the third cone before decelerating and walking back to the start and repeating the drill.

Key teaching points
- Maintain correct running form/mechanics
- Do not stop the arm drive to release the weights
- Keep the head tall
- Quality not quantity is vital

Sets and reps
3 sets of 4 reps, with 3 minutes' recovery between each set.

Variations/progressions
- On the release of the hand weights, the coach calls for a change of direction – i.e. the player is to accelerate off at different angles.
- Perform the drill backwards over the first 15 yards then turn, accelerate and release the weights to explode away.
- Perform the drill laterally over the first 15 yards then turn, accelerate and release the weights to explode away.

DRILL   *PARACHUTE RUNNING*

Aim
To develop explosive running over longer distances (sprint endurance) and explosive acceleration.

Area/equipment
Indoor or outdoor area – 4 cones and a parachute. Mark out a grid that is 50 yards in length. Place 1 cone down as a start marker, 1 at a distance of 30 yards, 1 at 40 yards and 1 at 50 yards from the start marker.

Description
Wearing the parachute, the player accelerates to the cone 40 yards away opening the parachute at the 30 yard point and then decelerates.

Key teaching points
- Maintain correct running form/mechanics
- Do not worry if, with the wind and the resistance, you feel as though you are being pulled from side to side. This will in fact improve your balance and co-ordination
- Do not lean into the run too much
- Quality not quantity is vital

Sets and reps
3 sets of 5 reps plus 1 contrast run, with a walk-back recovery between each rep and 3 minutes recovery between each set.

Variations/progressions
- Explosive re-acceleration. The parachutes have a release mechanism; the player accelerates to the 30-yard cone where he releases the parachute and explodes to the 40-yard cone before decelerating.
- Random change of direction – the coach stands behind the 30-yard cone. As the player releases the parachute, the coach indicates a change in the direction of the run. When mastered, the coach can then introduce the ball for players to run on to during the explosive phase.

DRILL BALL DROPS

Aim
To develop explosive reactions.

Area/equipment
Indoor or outdoor area – 1 or 2 balls.

Description
Working in pairs, one player drops the ball at various distances and angles from his partner. The ball is dropped from shoulder height; the partner explodes forwards immediately and attempts to catch or trap the ball before the second bounce. (Distances between players will differ because the height of the bounce will vary depending on the ground surface.)

Key teaching points
- Work off the balls of the feet – particularly prior to the drop
- Use a very explosive arm drive
- The initial steps should be short, fast and explosive
- At the take-off do not jump, stutter or hesitate
- Work on developing a smooth, one-movement run

Sets and reps
3 sets of 10 reps with a 2-minute recovery between each set.

Variations/progressions
- Player to hold 2 balls and to drop just 1 in order that partner anticipates and selectively reacts to 1 ball only.
- Working in groups of 3, with 2 of the players at different angles alternately dropping a ball for the third player to catch or trap. On achieving this, the player turns and accelerates away to catch or trap the second ball.
- Alter the start positions, e.g. sideways, backwards with a call, seated, etc.

DRILL UPHILL RUNS

Aim
To develop sprint endurance and explosive running.

Area/equipment
Outdoors. The hill should be approximately 20–40 yards in length with a gradient of no more than 4%. A few cones can be used to mark out various distances.

Description
Players accelerate up the hill over the nominated distance, and perform a slow jog back to the start position before repeating the drill.

Key teaching points
- Maintain correct running form/mechanics
- Ensure that a strong knee and arm drive are used
- Work at maximal effort
- Adequate recovery time between reps is essential
- Do not attempt to run up hills with steep gradients, as this will have a negative impact on the running mechanics

Sets and reps
3 sets of 6 reps with a jog-back recovery between reps and a 3-minute recovery between sets.

Variations/progressions
- Accelerate backwards over the initial few yards before turning to complete the drill as above.
- Overspeed – accelerate down the hill. Here control is vital!

DRILL MEDICINE BALL (JELLY BALL) WORKOUT

Aim
To develop explosive upper-body and core power.

Area/equipment
Indoor or outdoor area – Jelly Balls or medicine balls of various weights from 5–20 lb.

Description
Working in pairs, the players perform simple throws standing roughly 2 yards apart – e.g. chest passes, single-arm passes. They can also perform front slams, back slams, twist passes, woodchopper and granny throws by themselves (*see* photos).

Key teaching points
- Start with a lighter ball as a warm-up set
- Begin with simple movements first before progressing to twists, etc.
- Keep the spine straight and upright
- Take care when loading (catching) and unloading (throwing), as this can place stress on your lower back

Sets and reps
1 set of 12 reps of each drill, with a 1-minute recovery between each drill and 3 minutes recovery before the next exercise.

Variations/progressions
Long throw-ins – start by performing the throw-in with a normal ball. Then throw a Jelly Ball or medicine ball for 6 reps before performing a contrast throw with a light foam or plastic ball and then with a soccer ball.

Chest pass

Single-arm pass

MEDICINE BALL (JELLY BALL) WORKOUT cont.

Front slam

Back slam

Twist pass

Woodchopper

DRILL | SLED RUNNING

Aim
To develop explosive sprint endurance.

Area/equipment
Large outdoor grass area (preferable) – cones and a Sprint Sled. Mark out an area 30–60 yards in length.

Description
The player is connected to the sled and sprints over the nominated distance before recovering, turning around and repeating the drill.

Key teaching points
- Maintain correct running form/mechanics
- Maintain a strong arm drive
- Players will often need to use an exaggerated lean, to initiate the momentum required to get the sled moving
- As momentum picks up, the player should transfer into the correct running position

Sets and reps
2 sets of 5 reps plus 1 contrast run, with 1-minute recovery between each rep and 3 minutes' recovery between each set.

Variations/progressions
5-yard explosive acceleration – the player covers 50 yards by alternating between acceleration and deceleration phases over distances of 5 yards.

DRILL PLYOMETRICS "LOW-IMPACT QUICK JUMPS

Aim

To develop explosive power for running, jumping and changing direction.

Area/equipment

Indoor or outdoor area – Fast Foot Ladder or cones placed at 18" intervals.

Description

The player performs double-footed single jumps – i.e. 1 jump between each rung or cone (*see* fig. 5.6(a)). On reaching the end he turns around and jumps back.

Key teaching points

- Maintain correct jumping form/mechanics
- The emphasis is on the speed of the jumps, *not* the height
- Start slowly and increase the speed, but do not lose control (i.e. avoid feeling as though you are going to "fall over the edge of a cliff" when you reach the end of the drill)

Sets and reps

2 sets of 2 reps with 1 minute's recovery between each set.

Variations/progressions

- Backward jumps down the ladder or cones.
- Perform 2 jumps forwards and 1 jump back (*see* fig. 5.6(b)).
- Sideways jumps down the ladder or cones.
- Perform sideways jumps, 2 forwards and 1 back.
- Perform hopscotch – 2 feet in one square and then 2 feet outside the next square (similar to fig. 3.1(f), page 51).
- Perform left- and right-footed hops down the ladder or cones.
- Increase the intensity – replace the ladders or cones with 7–12" hurdles and perform the drills detailed above.

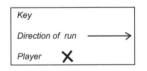

Key

Direction of run →

Player ✗

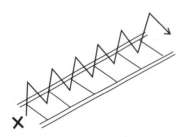

Figure 5.6(a) Low-impact, quick jumps

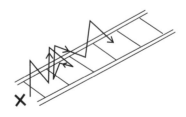

Figure 5.6(b) Low-impact quick jumps – 2 forwards and 1 back

DRILL PLYOMETRIC CIRCUIT

Aim
To develop explosive multi-directional speed, agility and quickness.

Area/equipment
Indoor or outdoor area – place ladders, hurdles and cones in a circuit formation (*see* fig. 5.7).

Description
The players jump, hop and zig-zag their way through the circuit as stipulated by the coach.

Key teaching points
- Maintain the correct mechanics for each part of the circuit
- Ensure that there is a smooth transfer from running to jumping movements and vice-versa

Sets and reps
5 circuits with 1 minute's recovery between each circuit.

Variations/progressions
Work in pairs, 1 player completing the circuit while their partner feeds them the ball at various points (i.e. to head, chest or kick as necessary).

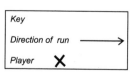

Key

Direction of run ——————→

Player   X

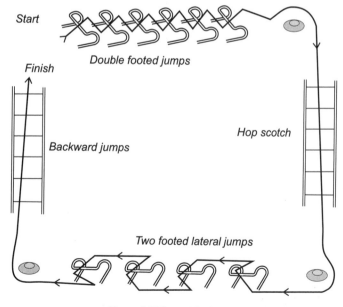

Figure 5.7 Plyometric circuit

DRILL DROP JUMPS

Aim
To develop explosive multi-directional speed.

Area/equipment
Indoor or outdoor area with a cushioned or grassed landing surface. A stable platform or bench to jump from of variable height – 15–36" depending on the stage in the season.

Description
The player stands on the platform and jumps off with their feet together, lands on the balls of the feet and then accelerates away for 5 yards.

Key teaching points
- Do not land flat-footed
- Do not sink into the hips on landing
- Maintain a strong core
- Keep the head up – this will help align the spine

Sets and reps
2 sets of 10 reps, with a 3-minute recovery between each set.

Variations/progressions
- Perform backward drop jumps, turning through 180° before sprinting off.
- Perform side drop jumps, turning and sprinting off.
- Perform drop jumps with a mid-air twist so that the player is facing the platform.
- Include a ball for the players to accelerate on to.

CHAPTER 6   EXPRESSION OF POTENTIAL

TEAM-GAMES IN PREPARATION FOR THE NEXT LEVEL

This stage is quite short in duration, but very important. Players bring together all the elements of the continuum into a highly competitive situation involving other players.

Short, high-intensity "tag" type games and random agility tests work really well here. The key is to fire up your players, for them to perform fast, explosive and controlled movements that leave them exhilarated – mentally and physically ready for the next stage of training or the game on Saturday.

DRILL   "BRITISH BULLDOG"

Aim
To practice multi-directional, explosive movements in a pressure situation.

Area/equipment
Outdoor or indoor area of approximately 20 square yards. Around 20 cones to mark out the starting and finishing lines.

Description
One player is nominated and situated in the center of the grid; the rest of the players stand at one side of the square. On the coach's call, all the players attempt to get to the opposite side of the square without being caught by the player in the middle. When the player in the middle captures another player, they then join him and work with him to help capture more "prisoners."

Key teaching points
■ Ensure that correct mechanics are used at all times
■ Ensure that all players keep their head and eyes up to avoid collisions with others

Sets and reps
Play "British Bulldog" for approximately 3–4 minutes before moving on to the more technical aspects of the game.

Variations/progressions
The player in the middle uses a ball to touch other players in order to capture them. The ball may be either kicked or thrown.

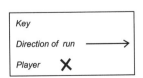

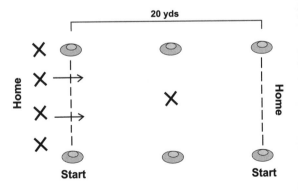

Figure 6.1 "British Bulldog"

DRILL CIRCLE BALL

Aim
To practice using explosive evasion skills.

Area/equipment
Outdoor or indoor area – players make a circle approximately 15 yards in diameter (depending on the size of the squad).

Description
One or two players stand in the center of the circle. Players on the outside have 1 or 2 balls. The object is for the players on the outside to try and make contact (by throwing the balls) with the players on the inside. The players on the inside try to avoid or dodge the balls. Those with the least number of hits during their "center phase" are the winners.

Key teaching points
■ Ensure that the central players use the correct mechanics

Sets and reps
Each pair to stay in the center area for 45 seconds.

Variations/progressions
■ Ball to be thrown, *not* kicked.
■ Players in the middle have to hold on to each other.

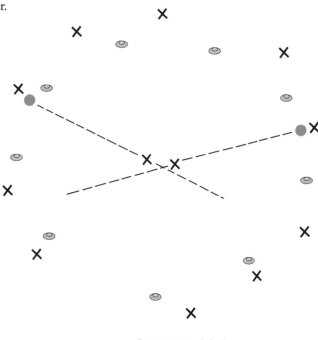

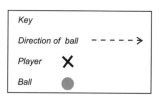

Figure 6.2 Circle ball

DRILL "ROBBING THE NEST"

Aim

To practice multi-directional, explosive speed, agility and quickness.

Area/equipment

Outdoor or indoor area – cones and balls. Mark out a 20-yard square area with a central circle of approximately 2 yards in diameter. Place a number of balls in the center circle.

Description

Two nominated players protect the nest of balls, with the rest of the players standing on the outsides of the square area. The game starts when the outside players all run in and try to steal the balls from the nest by dribbling to the outside or "safe" zone of the square. The two defenders of the nest try to prevent the robbers from getting the balls to the safe zone by stopping them with fair tackles. For every successful tackle, the ball is returned to the center circle.

Key teaching points

■ Ensure that correct mechanics are used by all players at all times
■ Encourage players to dodge, swerve, weave, side-step, etc.

Sets and reps

Each pair defends for approximately 45 seconds.

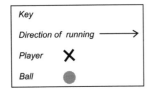

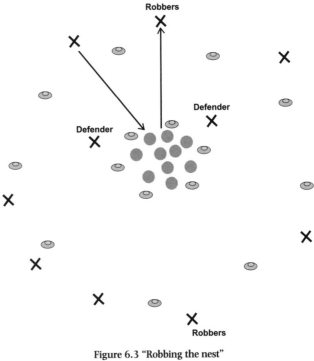

Figure 6.3 "Robbing the nest"

DRILL   ODD ONE OUT

Aim

To practice speed, agility and quickness in a competitive environment.

Area/equipment

Outdoor or indoor area – cones and balls. Mark out a circle of 20–25 yards in diameter and a center circle of approximately 2 yards in diameter. Place a number of balls in the center area. The number of balls should be one fewer than the number of players present.

Description

The players are situated on the outside of the larger circle. On the coach's call, the players start running around the larger circle. On the coach's second call they go and get a ball from the center circle as quickly as possible. The player who misses out is the odd man out and performs a ball-skill drill as directed by the coach. He retires from the game, the coach then removes another ball and the process is repeated.

Key teaching points

■ Ensure that correct mechanics are used at all times
■ Remind the players to be aware of the other players around them

Sets and reps

Play the game until a winner emerges.

Variations/progressions

Work in pairs – i.e. one ball between two players.

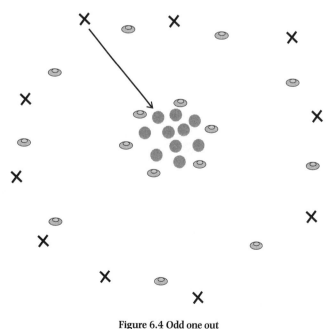

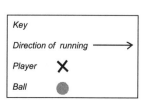

Key	
Direction of running	$\longrightarrow$
Player	**X**
Ball	●

Figure 6.4 Odd one out

DRILL CONE TURNS

Aim
To practice multi-directional speed, agility and quickness.

Area/equipment
Outdoor or indoor area – 50 small cone markers. Mark out an area approximately 20 yards square and place the cones in and around the grid; 25 of the cones should be turned upside-down.

Description
Working in two small teams (2–3 players), one team attempts to turn over the upright cones and the other team attempts to turn over the upside-down cones. The winner is the team that has the largest number of cones its way up.

Key teaching points
■ Ensure that players initiate good arm drive after turning a cone
■ Encourage players to use correct multi-directional mechanics
■ Be aware of other players around the area

Sets and reps
A game should last for about 60 seconds.

Variations/progressions
Use 4 teams and allocate 4 different-colored cones.

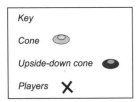

Key

Cone

Upside-down cone

Players X

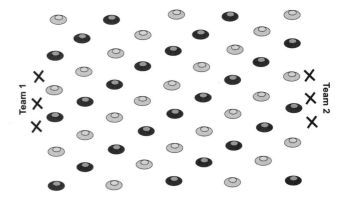

Figure 6.5 Cone turns

CHAPTER 7 POSITION-SPECIFIC DRILLS

In this section examples of position-specific patterns of movement are provided. By combining all areas of the SAQ Continuum – including techniques, equipment and drills – into game- and position-specific situations, you can improve and perfect the movement skills required by the players to succeed.

The primary aim is to improve the explosive speed, precision, control, power and co-ordination necessary for specific movements required by positions in all areas of the field. These are best introduced when the foundation work of SAQ has been mastered and during training sessions which are used to focus on the positional techniques of individual players.

DRILL *ATTACKING WING BACK DRILL*

Aim

To develop acceleration and speed of attack on the flanks, and speed and control of deceleration. To develop the control and agility required to jockey backwards, turn and accelerate back to defend.

Area/equipment

For maximum impact the drill should be performed in the relevant position on the pitch – 3 Fast Foot Ladders, balls and cones arranged as in fig. 7.1.

Description

The wing back accelerates down the first ladder, and passes the ball that is at the end infield to a waiting player or coach. The wingback then accelerates over 30 yards to the start of the next ladder, where he decelerates as he works his way up it. On leaving the second ladder, he crosses the ball that is at the end into the opposition's box. He then jockeys backwards for 10 yards (between the cones), keeping an eye on the result of the crossed ball, before turning and accelerating through the third ladder and sprinting back to the start cone.

Key teaching points

■ Concentrate on correct mechanics in all phases of sprinting, including acceleration and deceleration
■ Concentrate on the turn; this needs to be perfected as poor turns can cost 2–3 yards
■ Ensure correct techniques are used when the player is on the ball
■ Work both the left and right sides of the pitch

Sets and reps

6 reps with a 2-minute recovery between each rep.

Variations/progressions

■ Work in pairs with 1 player feeding the ball in at various stages throughout the drill.
■ Place cones in the 30-yard sprint area for swerves and zig-zags.

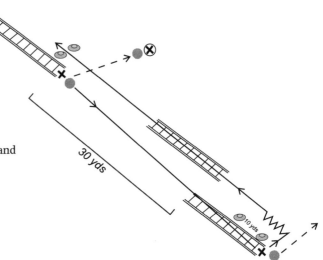

Figure 7.1 Attacking wing-back drill

POSITION – ALL DEFENDERS

DRILL **PRESSING A CLEARED BALL**

Aim

To develop the ability to defend the ball when it has been cleared from a dangerous position. This can be from crosses, set pieces and shots that require players to get the ball away quickly. To develop an understanding of the need to press and close down the space between players and the ball.

Area/equipment

For maximum impact the drill should be performed in the relevant position on the pitch – light hand weights and 8 cones marked out in the grid shown in fig. 7.2.

Description

The defender starts in a position between cones A and B, holding the hand weights. The coach calls the player to move forwards and backwards between the 2 cones. The coach then nominates 1 of the 6 outfield cones that represents where the ball has been cleared to. The player turns, accelerates and after the first 4–5 steps, drops the weights then explodes to the cone. On completion of the drill the player jogs back to the starting position.

Key teaching points

- Maintain correct running form/mechanics
- Use short steps and a strong arm drive when turning and accelerating
- Hand weights to be dropped as part of the running technique: do not stop or allow the arm mechanics to falter

Sets and reps

3 sets of 5 reps plus 1 contrast run with a 2-minute recovery between each set.

Variations/progressions

- Introduce jumping for the ball prior to the acceleration phase.
- Remove the outfield cones and replace with players. Each player is to have a ball and the defender presses the nominated player who takes the defender on.

Key

Player **✗**

Direction of running ⟶

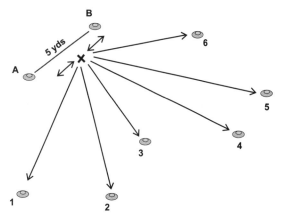

Figure 7.2 Pressing a cleared ball

POSITION – ALL DEFENDERS
DRILL   CUTTING ACROSS YOUR OPPONENT

Aim

A primary concern for a defender in front of goal is to get in front of and across the attacking opponent, cutting off their ball supply. This drill develops this skill with controlled explosion.

Area/equipment

For maximum impact the drill should be performed in the relevant position on the pitch – ball, cones and a Viper Belt with 2 flexi-cords attached, 1 to each side. Set the cones out as shown in fig. 7.3(a).

Description

Work in groups of 4, with player 1 wearing the Viper Belt. Player 2 holds a flexi-cord and stands directly behind player 1. Player 3 holds the other flexi-cord and stands to either the left or right of player 1. The fourth player stands further down the grid ready to deliver a ball (*see* fig. 7.3(b)). Player 1 accelerates down the grid; player 2 stands still and provides a resistance; player 3 runs laterally in line with player 1. When player 1 reaches the area between cone A and B they side-step towards cone D. Meanwhile, player 3 stands still at cone C to provide a lateral resistance. On reaching cone D, player 1 receives a ball delivered by player 4 that they head, chest or side-foot back. Player 1 then jockeys back to the starting position.

Key teaching points

■ Maintain correct running form/mechanics
■ When moving laterally, ensure that players do not skip, sink into the hips or allow their feet to cross
■ Encourage players to use small steps when moving laterally

Sets and reps

2 sets of 8 reps (4 moving to the left and 4 moving to the right), plus 1 contrast run with a 2-minute recovery between each set.

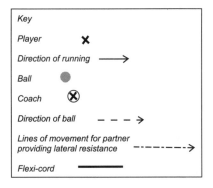

Key	
Player	**✗**
Direction of running	⟶
Ball	●
Coach	⊗
Direction of ball	– – – →
Lines of movement for partner providing lateral resistance	–·–·–·–·–→
Flexi-cord	▬▬▬

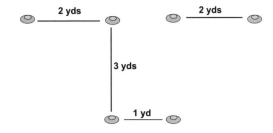

Figure 7.3(a) Cutting across opponent (grid)

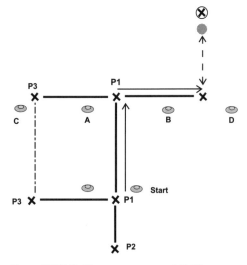

Figure 7.3(b) Cutting across opponent (drill)

POSITION – MIDFIELDERS

DRILL	*PALMER DRILL*

Aim

To develop speed, agility and control in a progressive center-field pressing drill – the object is to cut off attacking moves through the heart of the defense.

Area/equipment

For maximum impact the drill should be performed in the relevant position on the pitch – 2 Fast Foot Ladders and cones placed in the formation shown in fig. 7.4.

Description

The player accelerates down the ladder and moves explosively at the appropriate angle to the cone as nominated by the coach. Having reached the nominated cone the player jockeys backwards to the start/finish line.

Key teaching points

- Maintain correct running form/mechanics
- Develop awareness through the ladders by looking up
- Maintain an explosive arm drive during the change-in-direction phase
- Ensure that players work both to the left and right of the ladder

Sets and reps

1 set of 8 reps (coach should try to call 4 to the left and 4 to the right), with 15-second recovery interval between reps.

Variations/progressions

This variation involves the second ladder. The aim is to develop the center-half's explosive speed, and to close down an attacker who has decelerated early to draw the center-half out of defense. The timing is crucial! The center-half player accelerates down the first ladder and then sprints to the second ladder and decelerates down this one. On leaving the second ladder, the player moves explosively at the appropriate angle to the nominated cone, jockeys backwards for a few yards, turns and accelerates back to the start/finish line.

Key

Player	**✗**
Direction of running	
Turn	↻
Backward jockey	∧∧∧

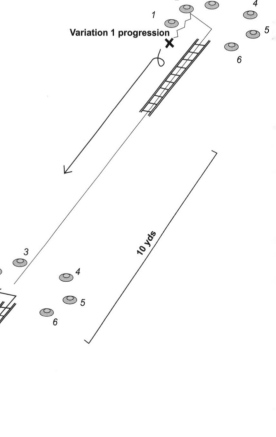

Figure 7.4 Palmer drill

POSITION – MIDFIELDERS

DRILL   BACKWARD TURN AND COVER

Aim

Teams may tactically attempt to bypass the midfield players by using the ball over the top. This requires the defensive midfielder to anticipate the direction of the pass by keeping an eye on the ball while covering backwards. When the pass is delivered, the player is required to turn, accelerate and cover. The speed of the turn and acceleration to cover is crucial!

Area/equipment

For maximum impact the drill should be performed in the relevant position on the pitch – 12 cones and a Viper Belt with a leash attachment (if you do not have a Viper Belt and leash, you can use a towel around the player's waist). Place the cones in a fan formation (as shown in fig. 7.5) with the outer cones representing the numbers on a clock face.

Description

Work in pairs, with player 1 wearing the Viper Belt and player 2 providing resistance by holding the leash attachment. Player 1 faces player 2 and moves backwards to a nominated inner cone. Player 2 provides some resistance but does go with player 1. On arriving at the cone, player 1 is released by player 2 letting go of the leash. Player 1 explodes into a turn and sprints to a nominated outer cone.

Key teaching points

- Maintain an upright position while moving backwards
- Use a strong arm drive while moving backwards
- On the turn, keep the feet shoulder-width apart – do not allow the feet to cross over
- After the turn, as the player comes into the linear position, encourage them to adopt an upright sprinting posture as soon as possible
- Player 2 should use short steps

Sets and reps

1 set of 6 reps, with a walk-back recovery between each rep and a 3-minute recovery before starting the next exercise.

Variations/progressions

- On player 1's release, the coach delivers a ball to an outer marker. The player must explode to the ball and retrieve it.
- A player with a ball moves between the outside cones. On the coach's call, player 1 turns, explodes and initiates a tackle on the player with the ball, whose aim is to beat player 1.

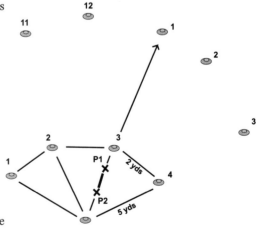

Figure 7.5 Backward turn and cover

POSITION – ATTACKING MIDFIELDERS

DRILL	*TURN AND ATTACK*

Aim

To develop explosive, precise turn-and-chase skills. Midfielders often face their own goal, waiting for the ball to be cleared by the defender or the goalkeeper. On many occasions the ball will go over the midfielder who will turn explosively, chase and regain the ball before setting up an attacking opportunity.

Area/equipment

For maximum impact the drill should be performed in the relevant position on the pitch – light hand weights and cones set up in a "Y" formation as shown in fig. 7.6.

Description

The midfielder holding the hand weights runs backwards for 5 yards. Without slowing down or changing mechanics, he then turns either to the left or right, and explodes to the first set of cones where the hand weights are released to allow the player to explode again to the outside cones.

Key teaching points

- Maintain correct mechanics when running backwards, turning and running forwards
- Increase the arm drive during the turn and acceleration phase
- Work off the balls of the feet, particularly when working backwards
- Release the arms without stopping or interrupting the arm mechanics

Key

Player   ✗

Direction of running ⟶

Sets and reps

2 sets of 6 reps, with a walk-back recovery between each rep and a 2-minute recovery between each set.

Variations/progressions

The midfielder works sideways for the first 5 yards, then turns and explodes. Ensure that the sideways foot movements are short steps and not skips.

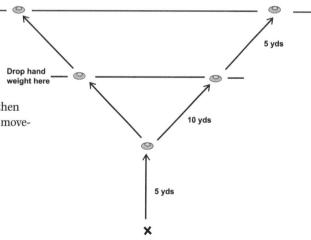

Figure 7.6 Turn and attack

DRILL

BALL CONTROL, FEED, TURN, RECEIVE, SHOOT

Aim

To develop explosive turning and running skills. The midfielder often receives the ball while he is facing his own goal and uses either his head, chest or feet to control it before quickly feeding it to a support player. The midfielder then turns and moves off at an angle to make himself available for the return pass that he receives before shooting at goal from 20–25 yards.

Area/equipment

For maximum impact the drill should be performed in the relevant position on the pitch – light hand weights and cones are placed as shown in fig. 7.7.

Description

Working in pairs, player 1 holds the hand weights and accelerates from cone A towards the center cone B. Player 2 at cone C delivers the ball to player 1; player 2 then moves off in an arcing run around either cone D or cone E. On receiving the ball, player 1 lays it off into the path of player 2's arcing run. Player 1 then turns explosively and accelerates down the center of the grid towards the goal/cones. After 5 yards, player 1 releases the weights, and player 2 passes the ball into the path of player 1 who explodes on to the ball and drives it into the goal.

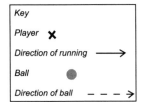

Key teaching points

- Maintain correct mechanics in all directional running
- Player 2 should use a powerful arm drive when making the arcing run – this helps their control
- Player 1 should use an explosive arm drive during the turn phase and must not allow his feet to cross
- Encourage verbal and non-verbal communication between the players

Sets and reps

1 set of 8 reps, with a walk-back recovery between each rep.

Variations/progressions

- Player 1 commences the drill by moving sideways for the first 5 yards.
- Player 2 also uses hand weights that are dropped halfway through the arced run.

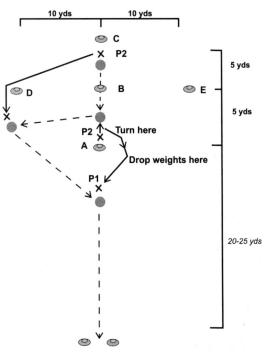

Figure 7.7 Ball control – feed the ball, turn, receive and shoot

POSITION – MIDFIELDERS

DRILL ASSISTED AND RESISTED ARCING

Aim
To develop timed, explosive arced runs into the defensive area. Attacking midfielders who run well-timed, angled or arced runs in and around the penalty area are very difficult for defenders to pick up.

Area/equipment
For maximum impact the drill should be performed in the relevant position on the pitch – 2 Viper Belts and cones. Place a cone down every 2 yards in an arc shape that is approximately 20 yards in length. Make several arcs and vary the directions and angles of these. (These should also vary from session to session.)

Description
Working in pairs, both players wear Viper Belts and are attached one in front of the other by a flexi-cord so that the lead runner is resisted from behind and the back runner is assisted by the lead runner. Standing at the start the lead runner sets off and runs along the cones. The flexi-cord will stretch after approximately 4–5 yards, at which point the back runner sets off. Alternate players between lead and back runner after each run and always finish a set with contrast runs.

Key teaching points
- Both players must maintain correct running form/mechanics
- The assisted player should lean into the assistance – do not lean back
- Do not stretch the flexi-cord more than three times its normal length

Key	
Direction of running	⟶
Flexi-cord	▬
Player	x

Sets and reps
1 set of 8 reps – i.e. 4 lead runs for each player, with 90 seconds' recovery between each rep and a 3-minute recovery before the next exercise.

Variations/progressions
The lead runner runs backwards and turns after the back runner has started their explosive phase.

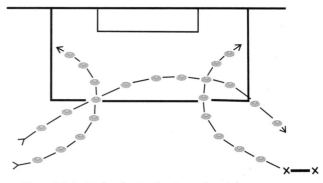

Figure 7.8 Assisted and resisted arcing and angled runs

POSITION – ATTACKING MIDFIELDERS

DRILL OVERSPEED ARC RUNNING

Aim

One of the best weapons for an attacking midfielder is the ability to run on explosive arcs into the penalty area. This makes the player difficult to stop and defend against.

Area/equipment

For maximum impact the drill should be performed in the relevant position on the pitch – an overspeed tow rope and cones. Set out the cones to make arcs of approximately 40 yards in length starting in the midfield and ending up somewhere in the penalty box.

Description

Players 1 and 2 are attached by the overspeed tow-rope belts. Player 1 is resisted from the front and player 2 from the back. Player 3 holds the handle and provides different levels of overspeed. Player 1 runs the arc, player 2 runs in a straight line away from player 3 who moves back towards the original start point of player 1. Player 3 must simultaneously keep an eye on player 1 to ensure that the right level of assistance is being provided.

Key teaching points

- Players 1 and 2 must use correct running form/mechanics
- Player 1 must relax – do not resist the power
- Player 1 should lean slightly into the pull, **not** against it
- Player 2 should take short, fast steps – do not sink into the hips
- Player 3 must keep an eye on player 1 – do not overload the power

Sets and reps

After 1 rep, rotate the players as follows: the resisted player becomes assisted, the assisted becomes player 3/control and player 3/control becomes the resisted player. Each player is to perform 5 reps.

Variations/progressions

Advanced – player 1 swerves in and out of some cones while running the arc.

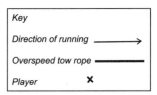

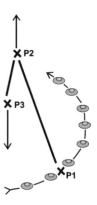

Figure 7.9 Overspeed arc running

POSITION – FORWARDS
DRILL **PEEL OFF AND TURN**

Aim
Forwards can have little space to work in, particularly when they are close to goal. The difference between scoring and missing can be a matter of inches; all forwards need to be explosive in all directions over the first 3–5 yards. This drill will help to develop the movements required when a player has their back to the goal and is closely marked. The player peels off quickly to get into the space vacated by the defender to receive a pass and shoot for goal.

Area/equipment
For maximum impact the drill should be performed in the relevant position on the pitch – Viper Belt and 3 cones marked out in a line 8 yards long (*see* fig 7.10) with a center cone 4 yards away from the start.

Description
Player 1 wears the Viper Belt loosely around his waist to allow him to turn within the belt, and stands on cone B. Player 2 holds the flexi-cord on cone A. Player 1 accelerates explosively towards cone C then swivels in the belt to explode back to cone A.

Key teaching points
- Use an explosive arm drive
- Use short, explosive steps during the turn
- After the turn, lean into the assistance – do not lean back

Sets and reps
2 sets of 6 reps plus 1 contrast run, with a walk-back recovery between reps and a 3-minute recovery between sets.

Variations/progressions
Player 2 has a ball and passes to player 1 as he explodes back towards cone A.

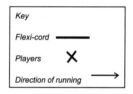

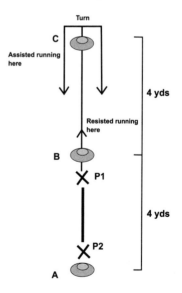

Figure 7.10 Peel off and turn

POSITION – FORWARDS
DRILL CROSS AND ATTACK GOAL

Aim

To develop short, explosive angled movements. Many forwards score goals by moving parallel to the goal then darting in through a gap to strike or head a ball crossed over the face of the goal. Sometimes only the tiniest of touches is required to put the ball in the net. This drill has been developed to add explosion to the initial sideways and backward movements that are used to confuse the defense, as well as the explosive, darting movement through a gap to contact the ball.

Area/equipment

For maximum impact the drill should be performed in the relevant position on the pitch – Viper belt with 2 flexi-cords attached front and back and 7 cones: Place 2 cones 7 yards apart on the 6-yard line in front of the goal, and the other 5 cones 2 yards in front and in a straight line (*see* fig. 7.11).

Description

Working in groups of 3, player 1 wears the Viper Belt with a flexi-cord attached at the front that is held by player 2. The second flexi-cord is attached at the back and held by player 3. Player 1 stands between the 2 cones on the 6-yard line, with players 2 and 3 standing on cones A and B respectively. On the coach's call, player 1 explodes the 2 yards to a nominated cone and then returns gently back to the start position for the next rep.

Key teaching points

- Work off the balls of the feet
- On the coach's call, use an explosive arm drive
- The initial steps should be kept short, precise and explosive
- The feet should be kept shoulder-width apart as much as possible. This is crucial just in case the player has to jump to contact the ball

Sets and reps

1 set of 8 reps plus 1 contrast run, with a walk-back recovery between reps and a 3-minute recovery before the next exercise.

Variations/progressions

- Vary player 1's starting position.
- Use a fourth player who nominates a cone for player 1 to explode to before feeding a ball at different angles and heights for player 1 to strike at goal.

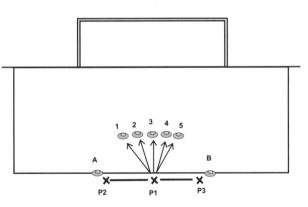

Figure 7.11 Moving across then attacking in towards the goal mouth

DRILL — POSITION – CENTRAL FORWARD
VERTICAL EXPLOSIVE HEADING POWER

Aim
To develop the ability of the center forward to jump as high as possible to meet crosses and direct them towards the goal.

Area/equipment
For maximum impact the drill should be performed in the relevant position on the pitch – Viper Belt with 3 flexi-cords (1 attached to each of the 3 anchor points) and 2 cones placed 7 yards apart in front of goal on the 6-yard line (*see* fig. 7.12).

Description
Players work in groups of 4. Player 1 (center forward) wears the Viper Belt and stands in a central position between cones A and B. Player 2 holds a flexi-cord on cone A and player 3 likewise at cone B. Player 4 has the third flexi-cord, which is attached to the back of the Viper Belt, and stands approximately 4 yards away from player 1 outside the 6-yard area (near the penalty spot). The coach throws the ball at different heights between player 1 and the goal-line for player 1 to head into the goal. Player 1 returns to the start position after each rep.

Key teaching points
■ Use explosive jump mechanics, especially arms for the take-off
■ Players 2, 3 and 4 should remain seated on the ground for the duration of the drill to increase the resistance
■ On landing, player 1 must not sink into the hips
■ Player 1 should try to stay upright and on the balls of the feet at all times

Sets and reps
1 set of 10 reps plus 2 contrast drills, with a walk-back recovery between reps and a 3-minute recovery before the next exercise.

Variations/progressions
Introduce defenders in front of player 1 to create a competitive jump/heading situation.

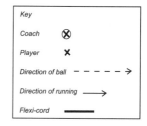

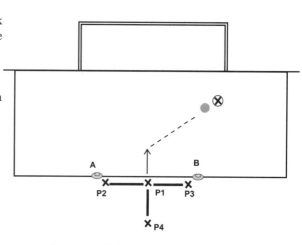

Figure 7.12 Vertical explosive heading power

SAQ Training for Goalkeepers

Recent research highlights the importance of specific conditioning being incorporated as a regular feature of a goalkeeper's training program.

Relying on standard training methods used by other outfield players fails to consider the specialist and specific conditioning required by this position. The demands placed on the goalkeeper are quite different from those placed on the outfield players. The ability to utilize the stretch and shortening cycle (*see* page ix) will have a positive impact on the explosive motion required while diving and springing into action.

Match analysis investigating the demands placed upon goalkeepers highlighted the following.

- 86% of playing time was spent walking or standing still.

- The remaining 14% of the time – the equivalent of 12 minutes – required the goalkeepers on average to make 13 saves or intercept a number of crosses, and make 23 short 4–5 m sprints.

- Many of the movements forwards, backwards and sideways indicated that a high level of multi-directional speed and agility were required.

Additional results indicate that most goals are conceded in the second half, or after periods of high-intensity work when the goalkeeper's explosive abilities have been fatigued. Therefore, the ability of the goalkeeper to remain explosive and multi-directional throughout the game is crucial. The flying dive to the bottom corner to fingertip the ball around the post is vital not only in the first but also in the last minute of the game. In the English Premiership, almost 70% of goals are scored in the bottom corners.

The following drills have been designed to ensure that goalkeepers become and remain explosive throughout the game.

POSITION – GOALKEEPER

DRILL NARROWING THE ANGLES

Aim

To develop explosive acceleration and speed, balance and agility over the first 5–10 yards. To assist the goalkeeper in narrowing the angle of players' runs towards the goal and to cut out through-passes.

Area/equipment

For maximum impact the drill should be performed in the relevant position on the pitch – 4 short ladders and 7–8 cones. Place the 4 ladders just inside the 6-yard area (*see* fig 7.13(a)), and the cones on the other side of the 6-yard line at different angles and distances of 5, 10 and 15 yards away from the ends of the ladders as shown.

Description

The coach nominates which ladder (A, B, C or D) the goalkeeper is to run down and which cone (1–8) they are to attack. The goalkeeper explodes down the ladder then angles off and accelerates to the nominated cone, where they set themselves for the save or dive.

Key teaching points

- The initial steps should be short and explosive
- Maintain a powerful arm drive
- Keep the head and eyes up
- Just before reaching the cone, the goalkeeper should extend his arms and make himself look "big"

Sets and reps

2 set of 6 reps, with a walk-back recovery between each rep and a 3-minute recovery between each set.

Variations/progressions

- Introduce a ball to make the drill more goalkeeper specific.
- Replace the cones with 1 or 2 players who move back and forth across the penalty area. The coach nominates the ladder for the goalkeeper to explode down; the goalkeeper then attempts to stop the outfield player who has just started his attack on goal.
- The goalkeeper wears a Viper Belt which is attached to their partner by a safety belt on the opposite end of the flexi-cord. The partner stands behind the goalkeeper and works with them but also creates a resistance throughout the drill.
- Place 6 short ladders in a semi-circle around the goalkeeper and repeat the drill (*see* fig. 7.13(b)).

NARROWING THE ANGLES cont.

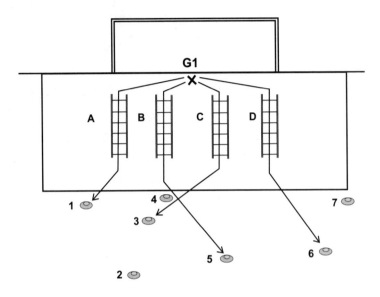

Figure 7.13(a) Explosive acceleration, narrowing the angles

Key

Direction of run ⟶

Goalkeeper ✗

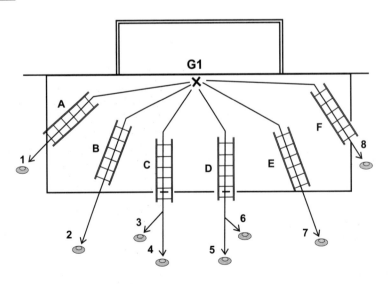

Figure 7.13(b) Explosive acceleration, narrowing the angles – variation

DRILL	**POSITION – GOALKEEPER**
	# LATERAL SPEED DEVELOPMENT

Aim

To develop fast, controlled lateral movement across the goal-mouth, making the goalkeeper difficult to get past and thus cutting down the options for the attacking players.

Area/equipment

For maximum impact the drill should be performed in the relevant position on the pitch – 2 ladders and 6 balls. Place the ladders just in front of the goal line, leaving a small space between them where the goalkeeper will stand (*see* fig. 7.14). Place the balls on a line parallel with the ladders, approximately 1 yard away.

Description

The goalkeeper stands between the 2 ladders. On the coach's call he commences lateral fast-foot drills (*see* pages 50–51) to either the left or right. The coach then nominates a ball (1, 2 or 3) and the goalkeeper explodes out of the ladder and on to the ball.

Key teaching points

■ Stay tall during the lateral drills
■ Use a few quick arm drives then revert to a "ready" position, i.e. extended arms and hands as if to save the ball
■ Keep the head and eyes up

Sets and reps

2 set of 6 reps, with a walk-back recovery between each rep and a 3-minute recovery between each set.

Variations/progressions

■ Position 2 players just outside the 6-yard area, 1 on each side. On the coach's call the goalkeeper and the relevant player both attack the same ball.
■ The goalkeeper wears a Viper Belt with 2 flexi-cords attached to players standing on either side of the goal in order to work the player under resistance.

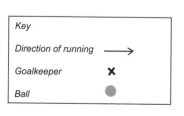

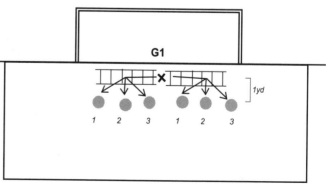

Figure 7.14 Lateral speed development

POSITION – GOALKEEPER
DRILL EXPLOSIVE DIVING

Aim
To develop multi-directional explosive diving – making the goalkeeper virtually unbeatable.

Area/equipment
For maximum impact the drill should be performed in the relevant position on the pitch – balls and a Viper Belt with 2 flexi-cords attached one on either side. The other end of the flexi-cord should be attached to either goalpost at waist height.

Description
The goalkeeper wears the belt and stands in the center of the goal. The coach stands with the balls in the center of the 6-yard line, then sends the balls towards the goal at different angles and heights. The goalkeeper attempts to save these by moving explosively in the appropriate direction before recovering, setting himself up again in position to repeat the drill.

Key teaching points
- The goalkeeper should use short and explosive steps
- Do not sink into the hips
- Stay tall and "big"
- Keep the head and eyes up
- Work off the balls of the feet at all times
- Keep the shoulders relaxed

Sets and reps
2 set of 10 reps plus 2 contrast saves, with a walk-back recovery between each rep and a 3-minute recovery between each set.

Variations/progressions
Introduce 2 saves per repetition.

Key	
Direction of ball	- - - - -
Flexi-cord	▬▬▬
Coach	⊗
Direction of diving	→
Goalkeeper	✗
Ball	⬤

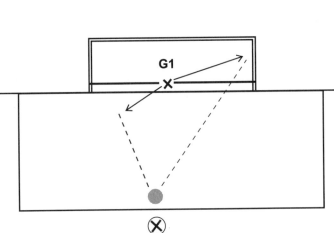

Figure 7.15 Explosive diving

DRILL **POSITION – GOALKEEPER**
ACCELERATION AND JUMP DRILL

Aim

To develop explosive speed over a short distance and an explosive vertical jump. The ability to do this will allow the goalkeeper to cut down space in danger areas and control balls crossed and floated into this area.

Area/equipment

For maximum impact the drill should be performed in the relevant position on the pitch – a Viper Belt with 2 flexi-cords attached one on either side, and 6 cones. Place 2 starting cones (A and B) 3 yards away from the goal line (*see* fig. 7.16). The remaining 4 cones are placed 3–4 yards away, i.e. on or just over the 6-yard line at different angles.

Description

Working in pairs the goalkeeper wears the Viper Belt and the other player stands behind the goal line holding both the flexi-cords. The coach then nominates a cone and the goalkeeper accelerates towards it. On reaching the cone he either dives or jumps into the air. On landing, he jockeys quickly back to the start position to await the next instruction.

Key teaching points

■ The goalkeeper should use short and explosive steps
■ The goalkeeper should stay tall and keep his head and eyes up
■ The player holding the flexi-cords should remain in a static, crouched position to increase the level of resistance

Key	
Flexi-cord	▬▬
Direction of running	⟶
Goalkeeper	✗

Sets and reps

2 set of 10 reps plus 2 contrast runs, with the backward jockey as the recovery between each rep and a 3-minute recovery between each set.

Variations/progressions

■ Work the goalkeeper laterally by turning the belt around and working sideways on to the cones. Ensure that the goalkeeper uses short, sharp steps and not skips.
■ At the nominated cone the goalkeeper makes 2 saves (1 high and 1 low) before jockeying backwards to the start position.

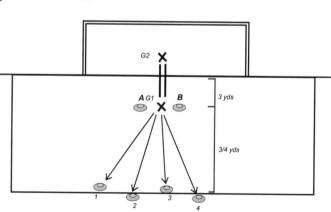

Figure 7.16 Resisted explosive acceleration and jump drill

DRILL

EXPLOSIVE GROUND REACTION

Aim

To develop explosive "get-ups" for goalkeepers who have just performed a save, are on the ground and have to get up as quickly as possible to initiate another save or block.

Area/equipment

For maximum impact the drill should be performed in the relevant position on the pitch – Jelly Balls (or medicine balls). Use various weights depending on the age group that you are working with. Seniors should use 15–24 lb balls.

Description

The goalkeeper lies on his back holding the Jelly Ball (or medicine ball) to his chest. On a call from the coach the goalkeeper simultaneously "gets up" and throws the ball away, finishing the drill in a ready position.

Key teaching points

■ Try to make the "get-up" one continuous movement (*see* page 69)
■ Try to get on to the balls of the feet as quickly as possible

Sets and reps

3 set of 10 reps plus 1 contrast without the Jelly Ball – with the return to the start position as the recovery between reps and a 3-minute recovery between each set.

Variations/progressions

■ Vary the start position, i.e side, knees, turn, etc.
■ Introduce a ball for the goalkeeper to save as soon as they have got to their feet.
■ Repeat the drill as above but with the goalkeeper sitting on an agility disc.

POSITION – GOALKEEPER

DRILL   EYE–HAND REACTION

Aim
To develop fast, accurate catching skills. To develop the goalkeeper's visual skills in following the ball in flight.

Area/equipment
Outdoor or indoor area – Visual Acuity Ring or a plastic hoop with 4 pieces of different colored tape attached at 4 equal intervals.

Description
Working in pairs approximately 5 yards apart, the ring is tossed so that it rotates through the air and is caught by the goalkeeper on the color nominated by the coach.

Key teaching points
- Keep the head still – move the eyes to track the ring
- Work off the balls of the feet at all times
- The hands should be out and in front of the body "ready" to catch the ring

Sets and reps
2 set of 20 reps with a 1-minute recovery between each set.

Variations/progressions
The goalkeeper starts with their back to their partner and on a shout turns to catch the ring.

POSITION – GOALKEEPER

DRILL **PERIPHERAL AWARENESS DRILL**

Aim
To develop peripheral awareness – this will help the goalkeeper to detect and react to the ball coming from behind and from the side more quickly.

Area/equipment
Outdoor or indoor area – Peripheral Vision Stick or a corner flag pole, or a stick or cane with colored tape on the end.

Description
Working in pairs, with 1 player behind the goalkeeper who stands in a ready position. The player holds the stick and moves it from behind the goalkeeper into his field of vision. As soon as the goalkeeper detects the stick he claps both hands over the ball at the end.

Key teaching points
- The goalkeeper should work off the balls of the feet and in a slightly crouched position with the hands out "ready"
- The player must be careful not to touch any part of the goalkeeper's body with the stick
- The player should vary the speed at which the stick is brought into the goalkeeper's field of vision

Sets and reps
2 set of 20 reps with no recovery between each rep and a 1-minute recovery between each set.

Variations/progressions
Instead of using a vision stick, throw balls from behind the goalkeeper that they have to fend off.

POSITION – GOALKEEPER
REACTION BALL DRILL
DRILL

Aim
To develop lightning-quick reactions.

Area/equipment
Outdoor or indoor area but not a grass surface – 1 Reaction Ball or a rugby ball.

Description
Working in pairs the goalkeepers stand 5 yards apart. One throws the ball so that it lands somewhere in front of the other goalkeeper; because of the shape of the ball it will bounce in all directions. The goalkeeper has to react and catch the ball before it bounces for a second time.

Key teaching points
- The goalkeeper should work off the balls of the feet and in a slightly crouched position with the hands out "ready"
- The ball should not be thrown hard – it will do the necessary work itself

Sets and reps
2 sets of 20 reps, with no recovery between each rep and a 1-minute recovery between each set.

Variations/progressions
- Goalkeepers can work individually or in pairs by throwing the ball against the wall.
- Goalkeepers stand on agility discs while throwing the ball to each other.

POSITION – GOALKEEPER

| DRILL | **BUNT BAT DRILL** |

Aim
To develop lightning-quick hand–eye co-ordination.

Area/equipment
Outdoor or indoor area – a Bunt Bat (or a stick with 3 different colored tapes positioned at each end and in the middle) and tennis balls or bean bags.

Description
Working in pairs, one of the goalkeepers holds the Bunt Bat. His partner stands approximately 3–4 yards away and throws a ball or bean bag and simultaneously calls the color of the ball on the Bunt Bat. The goalkeeper's task is to fend off the ball/bean bag with the appropriate colored ball on the Bunt Bat.

Key teaching points
- Start throwing the balls or bean bags slowly and gradually build up the speed
- The goalkeeper should be in a "set" position

Sets and reps
3 sets of 25 reps, with a 30-second recovery between each set.

Variations/progressions
- Use different-colored balls/bean bags – when the ball/bean bag has been thrown, it is to be fended off with the corresponding colored ball on the Bunt Bat.
- The goalkeeper stands on an agility disc while performing the drill.

Red   Blue   Green

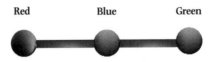

Figure 7.17 Bunt Bat

CHAPTER 8 WARM–DOWN AND RECOVERY

Due to the intense activity levels possible during the main part of the session, a warm-down should be performed to gradually bring the heart rate back to near resting levels. This will help to:

- disperse lactic acid

- prevent blood pooling in the lower body

- return the body systems to normal levels

- assist in recovery

The structure of the warm-down will essentially be the reverse of the Dynamic Flex warm-up and will last for approximately 5 minutes, depending on the fitness level of the players. It begins with moderate Dynamic Flex movements: these will gradually become less intense and smaller in amplitude (like a warm-up in reverse). These exercises should still focus on quality of movement – good mechanics.

Static stretches should then be incorporated. Carry out stretches that mirror the movements being carried out in the warm-down.

DRILL HIGH KNEE-LIFT SKIP

Follow the instructions given on page 8.

Aim
To warm down the hips and buttocks gradually.

Sets and reps
2 × 20 yards, 1 forwards and 1 backwards.

Intensity
60% for the first 20 yards and 50% for the second 20 yards.

DRILL KNEE-ACROSS SKIP

Follow the instructions on page 9.

Aim
To warm down the hip flexors gradually by lowering the intensity of the exercise.

Sets and reps
2 × 20 yards, 1 forwards and 1 backwards.

Intensity
50% for the first 20 yards and 40% for the second 20 yards.

DRILL WIDE SKIP

Follow the instructions on page 6.

Aim
To warm down the hips and ankles.

Sets and reps
2 × 20 yards, 1 forwards and 1 backwards.

Intensity
40% for the first 20 yards and 30% for the second 20 yards.

DRILL *CARIOCA*

Follow the instructions on page 19.

Aim
To warm down the hips and bring the core body temperature down.

Sets and reps
2 × 20 yards, 1 left leg leading and 1 right leg leading.

Intensity
30% for the first 20 yards and 20% for the second 20 yards.

DRILL *SMALL SKIPS*

Follow the instructions on page 5.

Aim
To warm down the muscles of the lower leg and the ankle.

Sets and reps
2 × 20 yards, 1 forwards and 1 backwards.

Intensity
20% for the first 20 yards and 10% for the second 20 yards.

DRILL *ANKLE FLICKS*

Follow the instructions on page 4.

Aim
To bring the heart rate down and to stretch the calf and the ankle.

Sets and reps
2 × 20 yards, 1 forwards and 1 backwards.

Intensity
10% for the first 20 yards and then walking flicks for the second 20 yards.

DRILL   *HURDLE WALK*

Follow the instructions on page 16.

Aim
To bring the heart rate down.

Sets and reps
2 × 20 yards, 1 forwards and 1 backwards.

Intensity
Walking.

DRILL   *WALKING HAMSTRING*

Follow the instructions on page 17.

Aim
To stretch the backs of the thighs.

Sets and reps
2 × 20 yards, 1 forwards and 1 backwards.

Intensity
Walking.

DRILL LATISSIMUS DORSI STRETCH

Aim
To stretch the muscles of the back.

Description
Stand in an upright position and link the hands together in front of the chest. Then push the hands out, straightening the arms and the back forwards.

Key teaching points
■ Do not force the arms out too far
■ Focus on slow, controlled breathing

Sets and reps
Hold the stretch for approximately 10 seconds.

DRILL QUADRICEPS STRETCH

Aim
To stretch and assist recovery of the muscles at the front of the thigh.

Description
Stand on one leg and bring the heel of the raised foot in towards the buttock. Using the hand of that side, hold the "lace" area of that foot and squeeze it into the buttock.

Key teaching points
■ Try to keep the knees together
■ Ensure the support leg is slightly bent. Repeat on the opposite leg
■ Press the hip forward
■ Focus on slow, controlled breathing
■ Do not force the stretch – just squeeze it in gently

Sets and reps
Hold the stretch for approximately 10 seconds on each leg.

Variation
The exercise can be performed while the player is lying down sideways on the floor.

DRILL HAMSTRING STRETCH

Aim
To stretch and assist the recovery of the hamstring at the back of the thigh.

Description
Sit on the floor with one leg extended and the other leg bent. Bend forwards from the hips and reach down towards the foot.

Key teaching points
- Focus on slow, controlled breathing
- Bend forwards from the hips
- Keep the back straight and flat
- Flex the foot to increase the stretch

Sets and reps
Hold the stretch for approximately 10 seconds on each leg.

DRILL ADDUCTORS STRETCH

Aim
To stretch and assist the recovery of the adductor muscles of the inner thigh.

Description
Stand with the legs apart, bend one knee and keep the foot at a 45° angle to the body, toes pointing ahead and knee over the ankle. The other leg should be straight. Repeat on the opposite leg.

Key teaching points
- Focus on slow, controlled breathing
- Do not force the stretch
- Keep the back straight
- Do not allow the knee of the bent leg to go forwards beyond the toes

Sets and reps
Hold the stretch for approximately 10 seconds on each leg.

DRILL CALF STRETCH

Aim
To stretch and assist the recovery of the calf muscles.

Area/equipment
Indoors or outdoors.

Description
Stand with the legs split and both feet pointing forwards, one leg to the front and the other to the back. The weight should be transferred to the knee of the front leg.

Key teaching points
- The front knee should only move to a position over the ankle, never beyond toward the toes
- The back leg should be kept straight; it is this calf that will be stretched. Repeat on the other side
- Focus on slow, controlled breathing
- Do not force the stretch
- Apply the weight slowly to the front foot

Sets and reps
Hold the stretch for approximately 10 seconds on each leg.

CHAPTER 9 THE SAQ SOCCER PROGRAM

The following chapter provides training session and program samples for both professional and amateur teams, with a focus on pre- and in-season sessions.

The art of any program is how it is periodized throughout the year, plus its ability to recognize individual needs and accommodate unscheduled changes. The best programs are those which have variation, provide challenges, keep players on their toes and accept individuality. Too much of the "same" demotivates individuals and teams, so that performance may be compromised.

Some Simple Rules

- Start with dynamic flexibility

- Explosive work and sprints should be completed early in the session, before endurance work

- Plan sessions so that an explosive day is followed by a preparation day

- Progress from simple to complex drills

- Don't restrict programs to one-week periods; work with different blocks of 4–8–10–12 days

- Teach one new skill a day

- Rest and recovery periods must be well planned

- Vary work-to-rest ratios in order to increase intensity of work rate

- Build up strength before performing plyometrics

- Keep sessions short and sharp. Explanation and discussions should be conducted before and afterwards, not in activity time

- Finish off each session with static stretching

Pre–Season Training

Mention the words "pre-season training" to most players and you will get a look of horror. For years, coaches and trainers have been fixated by the development of the aerobic energy system by utilizing long, slow, steady-state runs from 5 miles to anything up to 8 miles. In fact, research clearly shows that this type of activity is not suitable for soccer players – and is actually likely to make them slower and cause unnecessary injuries.

Most activity in soccer lasts for an average of 4–6 seconds, and for about 20–25 yards in distance. Soccer is a start–stop game, which utilizes fast-twitch muscle fibers and primarily depends on the anaerobic system (see Glossary, page 144). By training the anaerobic system via explosive drills like those in this program, players will benefit in a wide range of ways, including:

- an increased ability to tolerate higher levels of lactic acid – a by-product of high-intensity activity

- improved recovery time – both of which will enable them to play harder and for longer.

So it's simple – long, slow runs do not emulate what happens on the field; they are not specific to soccer. Instead, intermittent, intensive runs of various work–rest ratios – including side-steps, swerves, backward movements and jumps – better prepare your players for the demands of the game.

SAQ CONTINUUM	DRILLS	SETS AND REPS	EQUIPMENT	PLAN	TIME
Dynamic Flex	All with ball	Up and back – each drill	Cones and balls	Work in pairs over a 20-yard split grid. Perform a Dynamic Flex drill over the first part of the grid, pick the ball up and perform a ball-skill up and back over the second part of the grid. Return to the start by performing the drill backwards	18 mins
Mechanics	• Dead leg run • Lateral step • Single-leg lead Introduce the ball at the end of the grid	1 set of 6 reps of each drill without the ball, and then 1 set of 6 reps with the ball	8 hurdles, cones and balls	Place the hurdles in a straight line with approximately 18" between each hurdle	10 mins
Innervation	• Single step • Lateral step • Hopscotch • Icky shuffle Introduce the ball in the middle for passing skills	1 set of 6 reps of each drill	4 single ladders, 4 cones and 2 balls	Place the ladders in a cross-formation, leaving a space in the middle of approximately 3 square yards	12 mins
Accumulation of potential	A skill circuit incorporating mechanics drills, fast-feet drills and the ball	1 set of 6 reps	12 cones, 2 ladders and 12 hurdles	Place the ladders, hurdles and cones in a circuit to provide the player with the chance to practice zig-zag, lateral and linear runs forwards and backwards, as well as jump, turn and acceleration mechanics. Incorporate the ball where possible	10 mins
Explosion	• Out-and-back (include a pass) • Lateral side-stepping • Jockeying with Side-Steppers	1 set of 8 reps of each drill	Viper Belt, Side-Stepper, cones and balls	• Out-and-back – wearing a Viper Belt, work out and back to 3 angled cones approximately 2½ yards away • Zig-zag – wearing the Side-Steppers, work in a zig-zag pattern along the channel of cones that are approx. 2 yards apart • Wearing the Side-Steppers, jockey up and back along a 20-yard channel	18 mins
Expression of potential	• Odd-man-out • British Bulldog	1 game of approximately 3–4 minutes	Cones and a ball	Split the squad into 4 groups. Set up 2 games which can be played simultaneously – after the game, swap the teams around	8 mins
Warm-down	Dynamic Flex and static stretching	Up and back – each drill, and 10-second hold on static stretches	Cones	Work over a 20-yard grid for the dynamic flexibility, gradually decreasing the intensity of the drills	12 mins

Table 9.1 Typical SAQ soccer session

PROFESSIONAL AND AMATEUR PROGRAMS

Professional Program

The pre-season professional programs start with a higher percentage of time spent on running mechanics than explosive work. As the season draws closer the emphasis progressively changes with a higher percentage of time being spent on the explosive development and less on the mechanics.

By gradually shortening the recovery periods and increasing the intensity of the interval runs the program becomes more game-like in intensity. By incorporating competitive soccer conditioning teamwork exercises in the latter part of the pre-season program, the players are prepared for the psychological and physical demands of the forthcoming competitive season.

The professional in-season programs have been designed for use as a continuous top-up of the pre-season work already started. The importance of in-season programs is to ensure that the players remain fresh, motivated and match-fit.

Amateur Program

Training for amateur soccer differs from training for the professional game, predominantly in the amount of time available for preparation. Amateur players are part time and have to rely more heavily on personal training programs away from the club. This fact has been allowed for within the programs on the following pages.

The amateur pre-season programs also use interval-based training where the work, rest and recovery ratios can be manipulated by the coach. In this way the coach can ensure that at the end of the pre-season phase, a higher intensity of training has been achieved in preparation for the season itself.

As with the professional programs, the amateur in-season programs have been designed to keep the players match-fit, motivated and fresh for all games.

PRE–SEASON PROGRAM: PROFESSIONAL

T U E S D A Y

Dynamic Flex warm-up	20 min
MECHANICS Hurdles, Fast Foot Ladder drills To develop and perfect the correct linear, lateral and vertical movement mechanics. To increase foot speed and stride frequency.	15 min
SOCCER-SPECIFIC CONDITIONING **Innervation** Soccer-related movement drills: agility, speed, multi-directional. **Explosion** Resisted, random agility and assisted drills. To develop multi-directional speed. Ratio: mechanics, 70%; explosive, 30%. Active recovery.	25 min
SOCCER-SPECIFIC ENDURANCE Sprint endurance work. Example: 10×80 m, 8×60 m, 6×40 m. Timed active recovery.	20 min
COOL-DOWN/STATIC STRETCHING Preparation for afternoon session.	10 min
	TOTAL: 90 MIN

PRE–SEASON PROGRAM: PROFESSIONAL

W E D N E S D A Y

Dynamic Flex warm-up	20 min
MECHANICS	15 min
SOCCER-SPECIFIC CONDITIONING	25 min
Innervation Soccer related movement drills: agility, speed, multi-directional. **Explosion** Resisted, random agility and assisted drills. To develop explosive multi-directional speed. Ratio: mechanics, 70%; explosive, 30%. Active recovery.	
SOCCER-SPECIFIC ENDURANCE SAQ combination runs: 3 circuits – timed.	20 min
COOL-DOWN/STATIC STRETCHING	10 min
	TOTAL: 90 MIN

T H U R S D A Y

Dynamic Flex warm-up	20 min
MECHANICS	15 min
SOCCER-SPECIFIC CONDITIONING	25 min
Innervation Soccer-related movement drills: agility, speed, multi-directional. **Explosion** Resisted, random agility and assisted drills. To develop multi-directional speed. Ratio: mechanics, 70%; explosive, 30%. Active recovery.	
SOCCER-SPECIFIC ENDURANCE Sprint endurance work. Example: 10×80 m, 8×60 m, 6×40 m. Timed active recovery.	20 min
COOL-DOWN/STATIC STRETCHING	10 min
	TOTAL: 90 MIN

PRE–SEASON PROGRAM: PROFESSIONAL

FRIDAY

Dynamic Flex warm-up	20 min
MECHANICS	15 min
SOCCER-SPECIFIC CONDITIONING **Innervation** Soccer-related movement drills: agility, speed, multi-directional. **Explosion** Resisted, random agility and assisted drills. To develop explosive, multi-directional speed. Ratio: mechanics, 60%; explosive, 40%*. Active recovery.	25 min
SOCCER-SPECIFIC ENDURANCE SAQ combination runs: 3 circuits – timed.	20 min
COOL-DOWN/STATIC STRETCHING	10 min
	TOTAL: 90 MIN

Change in ratio of mechanics to explosive

SATURDAY

Dynamic Flex warm-up	20 min
MECHANICS	15 min
COMPETITIVE SOCCER CONDITIONING Group split into teams. Non-contact competitive soccer movements, drills, games and challenges to increase pressure. To develop sprints, reactions and increase enjoyment factor. Psychological impact: will increase competitiveness. ■ Relays ■ Obstacle courses ■ Competition games ■ Testing	40 min
COOL-DOWN/STATIC STRETCHING	10 min
	TOTAL: 85 MIN

SUNDAY AND MONDAY

Two-day recovery, personal stretching/swimming.

PRE–SEASON PROGRAM: PROFESSIONAL

TUESDAY

Dynamic Flex warm-up	20 min
MECHANICS	15 min
SOCCER-SPECIFIC CONDITIONING	25 min
Innervation Soccer-related movement drills: agility, speed, multi-directional. **Explosion** Resisted, random agility and assisted drills. To develop multi-directional speed. Ratio: mechanics, 60%; explosive, 40%. Active recovery.	
SOCCER-SPECIFIC ENDURANCE Sprint endurance work. Example: 10×80 m, 8×60 m, 6×40 m*.	20 min
COOL-DOWN/STATIC STRETCHING	10 min
	TOTAL: 90 MIN

Active recovery time reduced.

WEDNESDAY

Dynamic Flex warm-up	20 min
MECHANICS	15 min
SOCCER-SPECIFIC CONDITIONING	25 min
Innervation Soccer-related movement drills: agility, speed, multi-directional. **Explosion** Resisted, random agility and assisted drills. To develop explosive, multi-directional speed. Ratio: mechanics, 60%; explosive, 40%. Active recovery.	
SOCCER-SPECIFIC ENDURANCE SAQ combination runs: 4 circuits – each timed*.	20 min
COOL-DOWN/STATIC STRETCHING	10 min
	TOTAL: 90 MIN

Volume increased
Evening swimming pool session

PRE–SEASON PROGRAM: PROFESSIONAL

T H U R S D A Y

Dynamic Flex warm-up	20 min
MECHANICS	15 min
SOCCER-SPECIFIC CONDITIONING **Innervation** Soccer-related movement drills: agility, speed, multi-directional. **Explosion** Resisted, random agility and assisted drills. To develop multi-directional speed. Ratio: mechanics, 60%; explosive, 40%. Active recovery.	25 min
SOCCER-SPECIFIC ENDURANCE Sprint endurance work. Example: 11×80 m, 10×60 m, 8×40 m*. Timed, active recovery.	20 min
COOL-DOWN/STATIC STRETCHING	10 min
	TOTAL: 90 MIN

Sprint volume increased

F R I D A Y

Dynamic Flex warm-up	20 min
MECHANICS	15 min
SOCCER-SPECIFIC CONDITIONING **Innervation** Soccer-related movement drills: agility, speed, multi-directional. **Explosion** Resisted, random agility and assisted drills. To develop explosive, multi-directional speed. Ratio: mechanics, 50%; explosive 50%*. Active recovery.	25 min
SOCCER-SPECIFIC ENDURANCE SAQ combination run: 4 circuits – timed.	20 min
COOL-DOWN/STATIC STRETCHING	10 min
	TOTAL: 90 MIN

Change in ration of mechanics to explosive

PRE–SEASON PROGRAM: PROFESSIONAL

SATURDAY

Dynamic Flex warm-up	20 min
COMPETITIVE SOCCER CONDITIONING Group split into teams. Non-contact competitive soccer movements, drills, games and challenges will be used to increase pressure. To develop sprints, reactions and include enjoyment factor. Psychological impact: will increase competitiveness. ■ Relays ■ Obstacle courses ■ Competition games ■ Testing	40 min
COOL-DOWN/PNF STATIC STRETCHING	10 min
	TOTAL: 70 MIN

SUNDAY AND MONDAY

Two-day recovery, personal stretching/swimming.

PRE–SEASON PROGRAM: PROFESSIONAL

TUESDAY

Dynamic Flex warm-up	20 min
MECHANICS	15 min
SOCCER-SPECIFIC CONDITIONING	25 min
Innervation Soccer-related movement drills: agility, speed, multi-directional. **Explosion** Resisted, random agility and assisted drills will be used. To develop multi-directional speed. Ratio: mechanics, 50%; explosive, 50%. Active recovery	
SOCCER-SPECIFIC ENDURANCE Sprint endurance work. Example: 11×80 m, 10×60 m, 8×40 m. Active recovery time reduced.	20 min
COOL-DOWN/STATIC STRETCHING	10 min
	TOTAL: 90 MIN

WEDNESDAY

Dynamic Flex warm-up	20 min
MECHANICS	15 min
SOCCER-SPECIFIC CONDITIONING	25 min
Innervation Soccer related movement drills: agility, speed, multi-directional. **Explosion** Resisted, random agility and assisted drills will be used. To develop explosive, multi-directional speed. Ratio: mechanics, 40%; explosive, 60%*. Active recovery.	
SOCCER-SPECIFIC ENDURANCE SAQ combination run: 4 circuits – timed.	20 min
COOL-DOWN/STATIC STRETCHING	10 min
	TOTAL: 90 MIN

Change in ratio of mechanics to explosive

PRE–SEASON PROGRAM: PROFESSIONAL

THURSDAY

Dynamic Flex warm-up	20 min
MECHANICS	15 min
SOCCER-SPECIFIC CONDITIONING	25 min
Innervation Soccer-related movement drills: agility, speed, multi-directional. **Explosion** Resisted, random agility and assisted drills will be used. To develop multi-directional speed. Ratio: mechanics, 40%; explosive, 60%. Active recovery.	
SOCCER-SPECIFIC ENDURANCE Sprint endurance work. Example: 12×80 m, 10×60 m, 10×40 m. Sprints volume increased. Timed active recovery.	20 min
COOL-DOWN/STATIC STRETCHING	10 min
	TOTAL: 90 MIN

FRIDAY

Dynamic Flex warm-up	20 min
MECHANICS	15 min
SOCCER-SPECIFIC CONDITIONING	25 min
Innervation Soccer-related movement drills: agility, speed, multi-directional. **Explosion** Resisted, random agility and assisted drills will be used. To develop explosive, multi-directional speed. Ratio: mechanics, 40%; explosive, 60%. Active recovery.	
SOCCER-SPECIFIC ENDURANCE SAQ combination run: 4 circuits – timed.	20 min
COOL-DOWN/STATIC STRETCHING	10 min
	TOTAL: 90 MIN

Evening swimming pool session.

PRE–SEASON PROGRAM: PROFESSIONAL

S A T U R D A Y

Dynamic Flex warm-up	20 min
COMPETITIVE SOCCER CONDITIONING Group split into teams. Non-contact competitive soccer movements, drills, games and challenges will be used to increase pressure. To develop sprints, reactions and include enjoyment factor. Psychological impact: will increase competitiveness. ■ Relays ■ Obstacle courses ■ Competition games ■ Testing	40 min
COOL-DOWN/STATIC STRETCHING	10 min
	TOTAL: 70 MIN

S U N D A Y   A N D   M O N D A Y

Two-day recovery, personal stretching/swimming.

PRE–SEASON PROGRAM: PROFESSIONAL

T U E S D A Y

Dynamic Flex warm-up	20 min
MECHANICS	15 min
SOCCER-SPECIFIC CONDITIONING	25 min

Innervation
Soccer-related movement drills: agility, speed, multi-directional.

Explosion
Resisted, random agility and assisted drills will be used. To develop
multi-directional speed. Ratio: mechanics, 30%; explosive, 70%*.
Active recovery.

SOCCER-SPECIFIC ENDURANCE	20 min

Sprint endurance work. Example: 12×80 m, 10×60 m, 10×40 m.
Active recovery time reduced.

COOL-DOWN/STATIC STRETCHING	10 min
Change in ratio of mechanics to explosive	**TOTAL: 90 MIN**

W E D N E S D A Y

Dynamic Flex warm-up	20 min
MECHANICS	15 min
SOCCER-SPECIFIC CONDITIONING	25 min

Innervation
Soccer-related movement drills: agility, speed, multi-directional.

Explosion
Resisted, random agility and assisted drills will be used. To develop
explosive, multi-directional speed. Ratio: mechanics, 30%;
explosive, 70%. Active recovery.

SOCCER-SPECIFIC ENDURANCE	20 min

SAQ combination run: volume increased. * 5 circuits – timed.

COOL-DOWN/STATIC STRETCHING	10 min
	TOTAL: 90 MIN

Volume increased

PRE–SEASON PROGRAM: PROFESSIONAL

T H U R S D A Y

Dynamic Flex warm-up	20 min
MECHANICS	15 min
SOCCER-SPECIFIC CONDITIONING	25 min
Innervation Soccer-related movement drills: agility, speed, multi-directional. **Explosion** Resisted, random agility and assisted drills will be used. To develop multi-directional speed. Ratio: mechanics, 30%; explosive, 70%. Active recovery.	
SOCCER-SPECIFIC ENDURANCE Sprint endurance work. Example: 12×80 m, 12×60 m, 12×40 m*. Timed active recovery.	20 min
COOL-DOWN/STATIC STRETCHING	10 min
Sprint volume increased	**TOTAL: 90 MIN**

F R I D A Y

Dynamic Flex warm-up	20 min
MECHANICS	15 min
SOCCER-SPECIFIC CONDITIONING	25 min
Innervation Soccer-related movement drills: agility, speed, multi-directional. **Explosion** Resisted, random agility and assisted drills will be used. To develop explosive, multi-directional speed. Ratio: mechanics, 30%; explosive, 70%. Active recovery.	
SOCCER-SPECIFIC ENDURANCE SAQ combination run: 5 circuits – timed.	20 min
COOL-DOWN/STATIC STRETCHING	10 min
	TOTAL: 90 MIN

PRE–SEASON PROGRAM: PROFESSIONAL

SATURDAY

Dynamic Flex warm-up	20 min
COMPETITIVE SOCCER CONDITIONING Group split into teams. Non-contact competitive soccer movements, drills, games and challenges will be used to increase pressure. To develop sprints, reactions and include enjoyment factor. Psychological impact: will increase competitiveness. ■ Relays ■ Obstacle courses ■ Competition games ■ Testing	40 min
COOL-DOWN/STATIC STRETCHING	10 min
	TOTAL: 70 MIN

SUNDAY AND MONDAY

Two-day recovery, personal stretching/swimming.

IN–SEASON PROGRAM: PROFESSIONAL

S A T U R D A Y
OR ONE GAME A WEEK

All sessions start with Dynamic Flex

	A.M.		P.M.	
SUNDAY	Pool recovery, static stretching	45 min	Recovery	
MONDAY	**SAQ Session** Resistance work for power Ball work	90 min	Strength/power	45 min
TUESDAY	**SAQ Session** Fast feet Mechanics Agility Speed work Ball work	90 min	Recovery	
WEDNESDAY	**SAQ Session** Resistance work for power Ball work	90 min	Personal circuit conditioning	60 min
THURSDAY	**SAQ Session** Fast feet Mechanics Agility Ball work	75 min	Recovery	
FRIDAY	Dynamic Flex	15 min	Rest	
SATURDAY	Dynamic Flex, **game**, cool-down		Rejuvenate	

NB: *rest* – feet up and do nothing; *recovery* – active, low-intensity recovery e.g. swimming, walking, stretching, sauna, spa, massage; *rejuvenate* – immediately after game; refueling and re-hydrating.

IN–SEASON PROGRAM: PROFESSIONAL

TWO GAMES A WEEK

All sessions start with Dynamic Flex

	A.M.		P.M.	
SUNDAY	Pool recovery		Light ball work Stretching	45 min

MONDAY	Moderate strength/power
	SAQ Session
	  Agility
	  Fast feet
	  Ball work
		60 min	Light power	35 min

TUESDAY	Rest		Dynamic Flex warm-up to include fast feet work, **game**, cool-down and rejuvenate	
WEDNESDAY	Rejuvenate		Ball work	

THURSDAY	**SAQ Session**
	  Fast feet
	  Mechanics
	  Agility
		45 min	Personal circuit	45 min

FRIDAY	Dynamic Flex Light ball work	60 min	Rest	
SATURDAY	Dynamic Flex, **game**, cool-down		Rejuvenate	

PRE–SEASON PROGRAM: AMATEUR

1 4 - D A Y   C Y C L E

All sessions start with Dynamic Flex
(P) = Personal training session away from club

MONDAY	Weight-training program and flexibility work (**P**)	
TUESDAY	Dynamic Flex	15 min
	SAQ Session	40 min
	Interval work:	
	Combination run	5 min (2 min)
	Soccer drills	5 min (2 min)
	Combination run	5 min (2 min)
	Soccer drills	5 min (2 min)
	Combination run	5 min (2 min)
	Soccer drills	5 min (2 min)
	Abdominal workout and cool-down stretch	15 min total
WEDNESDAY	Active recovery: swimming, stretch (**P**)	
THURSDAY	Dynamic Flex with ball	15 min
	SAQ Session	40 min
	Power work with Jelly Balls/medicine balls	
	Interval running	5 min (2 min)
	Soccer drills	5 min (2 min)
	Interval running	5 min (2 min)
	Soccer drills	5 min (2 min)
	Interval running	5 min (2 min)
	Soccer drills	5 min (3 min)
	Cool-down stretch	15 min total
FRIDAY	Weight-training program	
	Stretch, swim, sauna (**P**)	
SATURDAY	Dynamic Flex with ball	15 min
	SAQ Session	
	Power development including recovery	40 min (3 min)
	Soccer drills	40 min (3 min)
	Soccer-specific runs	20 min
	Cool-down stretch then swim	15 min total + swim
SUNDAY	Stretch – rest	

NB: Time in parentheses indicates recovery period before moving on to next element of session.

MONDAY	Start own weight-training program and flexibility work (**P**)	
TUESDAY	Dynamic Flex	15 min
	SAQ Session	40 min
	Interval work:	
	Combination run	5 min (2 min)
	Soccer drills	5 min (2 min)
	Combination run	5 min (2 min)
	Soccer drills	5 min (2 min)
	Combination run	5 min (2 min)
	Soccer drills	5 min (2 min)
	Abdominal workout,	
	Cool-down and stretch	15 min total
WEDNESDAY	Active recovery: swimming, stretch	
THURSDAY	Dynamic Flex with ball	15 min
	SAQ Session	40 min
	Power work with Jelly Balls/Medicine balls	
	Interval running	5 min (2 min)
	Soccer drills	5 min (2 min)
	Interval running	5 min (2 min)
	Soccer drills	5 min (2 min)
	Interval running	5 min (2 min)
	Soccer drills	5 min (3 min)
	Cool-down and stretch	
FRIDAY	Rest	
SATURDAY	Dynamic Flex with ball	15 min
	SAQ Session	
	Power development including recovery	40 min (3 min)
	Soccer drills	40 min (3 min)
	Soccer-specific runs	20 min
	Cool-down, stretch off then swim	15 min total plus swim
SUNDAY	Stretch – rest	

Repeat 14-day program, reducing recovery times by 20 seconds in the first week and up to 30 seconds in the second week.

IN–SEASON PROGRAM: AMATEUR

All sessions start with Dynamic Flex

SUNDAY	Rejuvenate/pool recovery	
MONDAY	**SAQ Session** Team ball work Multi-sprints	90 min
TUESDAY	Individual strength and power program	40 min
WEDNESDAY	**SAQ Session** Team ball work Strength/power work Start complex carbohydrate load for Saturday's game	90 min
THURSDAY	Individual circuit conditioning	40 min
FRIDAY	Warm-up, light ball team-work Rest	75 min
SATURDAY	Warm-up, **game**, cool-down, refuel	

References

Gleim, G.W. and McHugh, M.P. (1997) "Flexibility and its effects on sports injury and performance," *Sports Medicine*, 24(5): pp. 289–299.

Pope, R. (1999) "Skip the warm up," *New Scientist*, Vol. 164, No. 2214, (18/12/99): p. 23.

Smythe, R. (2000) "Acts of agility," *Training and Conditioning*, Vol . V. No. 4, pp. 22–25.

Whall, R. (2000) "Conditioning the goalkeeper – a scientific approach," University of Liverpool, 1991.

Glossary

Acceleration	Increasing velocity, specifically over the first 5 yards.
Aerobic	System that uses oxygen to release energy.
Agility	The ability to change body position quickly and accurately in any direction without losing balance.
Anaerobic	Energy systems that do not require oxygen to function. Utilized during high intensity exercise of a short duration.
Competitive skills	Skills such as running, jumping or lateral movement that can be used in the sporting environment.
Contrast	A stage after the resistance phase where the player/athlete performs the same drill but unresisted.
Dynamic	Any movement, particularly a stretch, that actively moves a limb through its full range of motion.
Explosive movement	The ability to generate great amounts of force in a very short amount of time.
Flexibility	The ability to move a joint smoothly through its complete range of motion.
Force application	Ability to generate force from many small forces large enough to complete a specific movement or action, e.g. throwing a ball.
Goals	An important part of mental preparation in which the player decides and thinks about what he wants to achieve.

Hops	Single-leg repeated movements.
Jumps	Double-leg repeated movements.
Lactate	Leftover by-product of anaerobic metabolism that is converted back into ATP.
Lateral movement	A shoulder-leading sideways motion.
Linear movement	A forwards motion.
Maximum speed	Fastest speed achievable by an individual, usually reached between 30–50 yards.
Muscular efficiency	Utilizing muscle energy stores in a manner that is not wasteful to the athlete. Achieved by minimizing and eliminating unnecessary movements.
Neuromuscular recruitment	Activities that work to activate more muscle units.
Peripheral vision	Ability to see objects or movements at the "edge" of vision, or while focusing on other objects.
Plyometrics	Exercises, including hops, bounds and jumps, in which maximum effort is expended while a muscle group is lengthening.
Power output	The rate at which work is done.
Progressive overload	In training, constantly forcing the body to adapt to new stresses.
Quickness	The ability to generate a movement in a short amount of time.
Resistance	A type of training that involves tools to increase the force required to initiate and sustain movement.
Specificity	Training precisely for the demands of a specific sport or skill development.
Speed	The ability to move fast over a specific distance.
Strength	The ability to apply a force and overcome a resistance.
Velocity	Speed of motion.

Index of drills

Speed, Agility & Quickness International Limited International Trademarks

"SAQ"® Britain and Northern Ireland No. 2156613
"SAQ"® European Community No. 001026277
"SAQ Speed, Agility, Quickness"® Australia

SAQ™
SAQ Programs™
SAQ Equipment™
SAQ Training™
SAQ Accreditation Awards™

Fast Foot™ Ladder
Viper Belt™
SAQ Continuum™
Jelly Balls™
Micro Hurdles™
Macro Hurdles™
Speed Resistor™
Sprint Sled™
Power Harness™
Sonic Chute™
Agility Disc™
Side Strike®
Flexi-cord™
Velocity Builder™
Heel Lifter™
Visual Acuity Ring™
Peripheral Vision Stick™
Break Away Belt™ and Tri-Break Away Belt™
Dynamic Flex™
Bunt Bat™

The SAQ Continuum, SAQ Training, SAQ Programs, SAQ Accreditation Awards and SAQ Equipment are products and services of Speed, Agility & Quickness International Limited (SAQ International) and its licensees. Only individual or corporate holders of valid SAQ Trainer certificates or valid SAQ Training licenses issued by SAQ International may offer products or services under the SAQ brand name or logo (subject to terms).

Discover more about SAQ Programs, SAQ Accreditation Awards and SAQ Equipment online at www.saqinternational.com.